T0003927

A
Witch's
GUIDE TO
CREATING
&
PERFORMING
RITUALS
That Actually Work

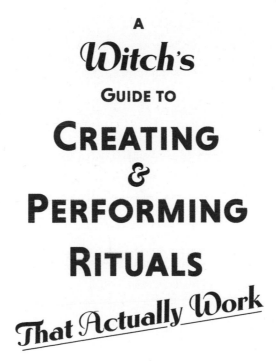

© Jessamyn Harris

About the Author

Phoenix LeFae (Sebastopol, CA) is a professional reader, rootworker, teacher, and ritualist. She has been practicing Witchcraft for almost thirty years, and her teachings are connected to the Reclaiming Tradition, Druidry, and Gardnerian Wicca. She is also the owner of an esoteric Goddess shop called Milk & Honey.

Other Books by Phoenix LeFae

Cash Box Conjure

Hoodoo Shrines and Altars

Life Ritualized

Walking in Beauty

What Is Remembered Lives

Witches, Heretics & Warrior Women

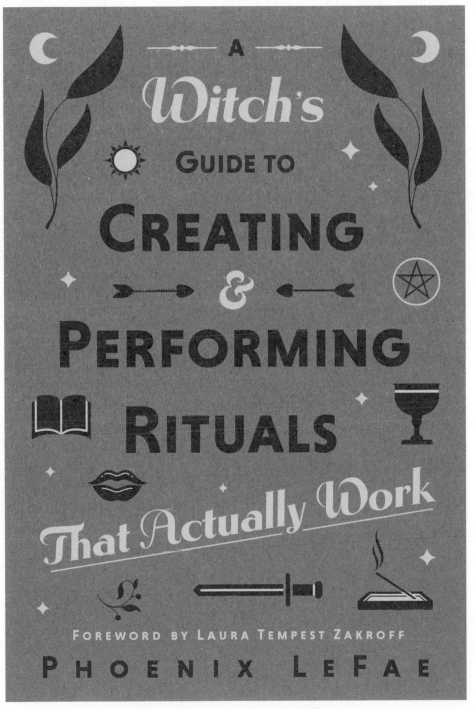

A Witch's Guide to

Creating

&

Performing Rituals

That Actually Work

Foreword by Laura Tempest Zakroff

PHOENIX LeFae

Llewellyn Publications • Woodbury, Minnesota

A Witch's Guide to Creating & Performing Rituals: That Actually Work © 2023 by Phoenix LeFae. All rights reserved. No part of this book may be used or reproduced in any manner whatsoever, including internet usage, without written permission from Llewellyn Publications, except in the case of brief quotations embodied in critical articles and reviews.

FIRST EDITION
First Printing, 2023

Book design by Mandie Brasington
Cover design by Kevin R. Brown
Interior art by Llewellyn Art Department

Llewellyn Publications is a registered trademark of Llewellyn Worldwide Ltd.

Library of Congress Cataloging-in-Publication Data (Pending)
ISBN: 978-0-7387-7141-0

Llewellyn Worldwide Ltd. does not participate in, endorse, or have any authority or responsibility concerning private business transactions between our authors and the public.

All mail addressed to the author is forwarded but the publisher cannot, unless specifically instructed by the author, give out an address or phone number.

Any internet references contained in this work are current at publication time, but the publisher cannot guarantee that a specific location will continue to be maintained. Please refer to the publisher's website for links to authors' websites and other sources.

Llewellyn Publications
A Division of Llewellyn Worldwide Ltd.
2143 Wooddale Drive
Woodbury, MN 55125-2989
www.llewellyn.com

Printed in the United States of America

This book is dedicated to Rose May Dance

Contents

Disclaimer

Witchcraft, ritual, and magick can do a lot to help improve your life, but that doesn't mean you should ignore medical care, stop taking medications, or bypass medical treatment. This book is not a substitute for any medications or medical care you are currently receiving or need.

You are ultimately responsible for all decisions pertaining to your health. Each individual's needs and restrictions are unique. The author and publisher are not responsible for adverse reactions, effects, or consequences resulting from the use of any suggestions herein.

There are herbs, oil, and potions suggested in this book. Do not use any of them if you are allergic to any of the suggested ingredients. If you are uncertain if you'll have an allergic reaction, then just don't use them.

If you find yourself struggling with your mental health or need help beyond the realm of Witchcraft, please seek help. This could include things like medical treatment, therapy, prioritizing your physical safety, and help with substance abuse issues. Remember, you are not alone. For a list of resources, see the back of this book.

Foreword

There are a handful of people in this world that I know if we were tasked with creating a ritual experience together, we could truly make magic happen at a moment's notice. Phoenix LeFae is absolutely on that esteemed list of magical folks I can always count on.

I've had the honor of working with Phoenix multiple times—often on the premise of one of us going, "Hey, I have this crazy ritual idea, do you want to do a thing at this big upcoming event?" Despite living nowhere near each other, coming from different traditions, and both of us being insanely busy, we have put together rituals that people are still talking about years after the fact. (In the good way, not the infamous way...) Whether it's crafting a ritual from scratch or stepping in to help mutual friends in their workings at the last minute, there's a sense of confidence and creativity that's always in the mix. The synergy that happens in a ritual where everyone's working at that level is simply amazing, beautiful, and powerful.

Yet you've also probably heard of, or even experienced firsthand for yourself, ritual that just didn't quite hit the mark. It might have been way too long or seemed too short, felt awkward or offensive in some way, was hard to follow, or just fell flat. Those negative experiences might make you shy away from working with others, attending community rituals, or even trying things for yourself. Which is fair—no one wants to be subjected to bad ritual. But how do *you* make it better?

Ritual is a very misunderstood entity. It's everywhere, all around us, and part of our daily lives. Yet when most people think of ritual, they tend to picture complicated and intricate ceremonies—often rehearsed, solemn, and oh-so-serious. This limited view of ritual not only makes many magical practitioners feel intimidated when tasked with creating or doing a ritual, it also inflicts lackluster rituals on others. But it doesn't have to be that way at all! The art of crafting and performing ritual should instill confidence, bring inspiration, and enhance the experience of everyone involved.

Ritual is life. Life is ritual. Our lived experience is composed of many big and little rituals that, together, express our paths and who we are. Humans are ritualistic beings, right down to the core of our blood, breath, and bone. Every day, we weave patterns to keep the pulse and rhythm of our lives flowing. We tap into ritual to celebrate the big moments too: sorrows and joys, accomplishments and changes, beginnings and endings, mysteries and revelations. Ritual helps bring meaning and order to daily living and inspires us to connect more fully to the world around us.

Yet even though we're immersed in all kinds of rituals throughout our lives, we can still be intimidated when tasked with consciously creating ritual. In this blessing of a book, Phoenix makes the crafting of ritual incredibly accessible and firmly guides you to be more intuitive in your approach. Within the following pages is everything you need to conceive, create, and perform ritual that will be powerful, effective, and memorable—for all of the right reasons!

This book is an essential guide that you will be referring to for years to come. I can already see the pages worn from use and full of bookmarks on your shelf. I'm especially excited that one day I might get to attend a ritual that you're doing at the next big thing—and I know it's going to be a wonderful experience because of Phoenix's working wisdom that you're about to discover.

Blessings on your path—may you be inspired!

—Laura Tempest Zakroff,
author of *Anatomy of a Witch* and *Weave the Liminal*

Introduction

At the age of fifteen, I stood in front of my bedroom window with the full moon's light shining down on me. My legs were firmly planted on the brown carpet and my arms were raised in a V shape above my head. I had a wooden-handled butter knife in my left hand, and there was an open book on the floor in front of me. It was the first moment that I felt like I was practicing Witchcraft.

The wind wasn't blowing through my hair. There wasn't an otherworldly glow in the room. There wasn't the sound of angels singing or anything like that. But it was one of the most magickal moments of my life. And it led me down a road of exploring rituals for the next thirty years.

The word *ritual* refers to a series of actions performed according to a prescribed order. Doesn't sound very magickal, does it? We perform a lot of rituals in our lives. Cooking dinner, brushing our teeth in the morning, driving to work; these are all typical daily rituals. But I'm guessing that you didn't pick up this book to learn about the ritual of brushing your teeth or driving a car. I know what you're thinking: *Isn't this book supposed to be about magick?* Perhaps you picked up this book hoping to read more about the rituals that are a little more Witchy in nature?

Picture this: It's late at night and there are dozens of candles casting a glow across the ritual space. There is sweet incense burning, leaving a light fog in the air that surrounds you and sticks to your skin. The smoke blurs your vision and shifts your awareness, just the tiniest bit. You can hear a rhythmic drumming coming from somewhere in the background. People, painted and wearing horns and earthy colors, are gathered in a circle. There is an energy in the air—a tingle, a sizzle, a feeling of *magick*. It is something ineffable, exciting, and maybe even a little bit scary. The ritual is about to begin, and the world will be transformed.

This scenario is a little more interesting than the image of standing at your bathroom sink scrubbing your teeth with a little brush and peppermint paste. Wouldn't you agree?

And yet, both of these types of rituals are magickal and worthy of our time and discussion. Both of these types of rituals are what we are going to explore in this book.

A Witch's life is a magickal life. So that means everything from drinking your morning coffee to drawing down the moon are rituals that we should honor. All it takes is a little awareness and a shift in our intention and approach to make something a ritual. Don't worry, we will get into all of this more deeply a little further along.

Humans have been creating rituals longer than we have been writing language down. It pains me to think of all the rituals that have been lost to the ravages of time because they were only handed down verbally from person to person. Rituals speak to us in ways that words aren't capable of. And to live a full and healthy human existence, we really do need rituals.

Rituals give us the time and space to process the things going on in our lives. To be clear, processing doesn't mean sitting on the couch crying with a pint of ice cream, thinking and stressing about the situation you have just been through. Although the ice cream might be soothing and helpful, or numbing and distracting, it isn't *processing* the situation. True processing is what allows you to move something through your body, your spirit, your being. True processing helps you deal.

Let me be clear, when I say move *something*, I am talking about an experience, a feeling, a need. *Something* could be joyous or harrowing. *Something* could be traumatic or celebratory. *Something* could be a holiday celebration or honoring the death of a loved one. *Something* is the thing that needs to be moved through your body, mind, and spirit. Just thinking about it, stressing about it, or avoiding it won't do. Through ritual, you have the opportunity to find peace, reclaim power, resolve issues, and maybe even move on.

Performing rituals isn't a foreign thing for us humans, even if you've never performed or participated in a formal rite before. Rituals are a part of our breath, blood, and bone. They are a part of our human makeup. Rituals do not belong to any one religion, and secular rituals can be just as powerful as religious ones.

The first Witchcraft ritual I ever performed was read directly out of a book in the mid-1990s. It was a rite from the book *To Ride a Silver Broomstick* by Silver Ravenwolf. I performed this ritual in the bedroom of my parent's house, whispering so no one would hear me. The ritual was sweet and simple. I read the words written by another Witch and felt connected to a magickal current bigger than myself.

A year or so later, I attended a public ritual for the winter solstice put on by Starhawk and the Reclaiming tradition of Witchcraft. There were close to a hundred Witches at this ritual. The Priestexes (I use Priestex as a more gender-inclusive term for Priest or Priestess) performed beautiful and thought-provoking invocations. We were led on a deep guided meditation, and then there was a spiral dance. One hundred Witches, singing and dancing together, accompanied by ritual drummers.

It. Was. Amazing.

All of the rituals I had done in my bedroom paled in comparison to this moment. I felt ecstatic. I felt alive. I felt like I finally knew what it meant to be a Witch. I wanted more, and I wanted everyone in the world to know this feeling.

After that, I started crafting my own rituals. I've put together, or helped put together, rituals for one to two people, a dozen or so folks, and hundreds of people. A ritual for an individual won't work the same as a ritual for one hundred people. There is a skill to creating and executing rituals, and it does take practice.

I started out by performing rituals straight out of books in my teens. In my early twenties, I began inviting coworkers over to my apartment for full moon craft nights, which led to running a dysfunctional coven with my friends for many years. Then I joined a Druid order where the elders ran everything and my role was purely that of a student. From there I got deeply involved with the Reclaiming tradition of Witchcraft, where every ritual is unique, collaborative, and ecstatic. Later, I was initiated into Gardnerian Wicca, where I hold a second degree. Throughout all of this, I have kept a solitary practice completely on my own.

My background has given me the opportunity to learn a lot about Witchcraft, ritual, magick—and what works in ritual, and what really doesn't work. Ritual is an art and a science, which means it is something anyone can learn.

Not all rituals work. I've had some major flops. But learning why a ritual flopped can provide a lot of information about how to do it better the next time. We will talk a lot more about this in the coming pages.

So buckle up, dear Witch. We are headed on an adventure of magick and mystery. Let's go!

Why Do Ritual?

Rituals can change your life and bring in more magick and mystery. And the truth is, our modern world really needs more mystery.

Rituals can:

- ◆ Help create stronger bonds with other people.
- ◆ Bring you more confidence and self-assurance.
- ◆ Help you process challenging events or moments.
- ◆ Help you celebrate transformative events or moments.
- ◆ Create time and space to process difficult emotions.
- ◆ Help you find gratitude for mystery.
- ◆ Bring structure into your day.
- ◆ Connect you with a power that is bigger than yourself.
- ◆ Give you space for health and healing.

In the Witchcraft and Pagan world, there are a lot of rituals that happen in specific traditions or public spaces where it feels like a High Priestess (HPS), High Priest (HP), or ritual facilitator is the one doing all the work. Sometimes these rituals can feel like you are *watching* a ritual rather than *participating* in one. My belief is that a ritual where everyone is participating creates an opportunity for a more powerful and transformative experience.

And it's important to remember that rituals don't belong to Witchcraft or Paganism—rituals are a part of all religions and secular life. However, in this book we will be focusing on the rituals of Witchcraft and how to create rituals that most would recognize as being under the umbrella of Witchcraft. So first, what is Witchcraft?

Witchcraft

Thirty years ago, it would have been relatively easy for me to explain what Witchcraft is. Things have shifted and grown so much over the last few decades that it's not so easy anymore.

There are a lot of different traditions of Witchcraft out there. There are a lot of different practitioners who all do things in different ways, and they all call what they do Witchcraft. There are thousands of social media accounts that excitedly show you the specific steps to practice their form of Witchcraft. What is both beautiful and maddening is that there isn't just one way to *do* Witchcraft. There is no "one true path." (And if you come across someone saying what they do is right and everyone else is wrong, run for the hills.)

Witchcraft is the practice of magick, or a religious practice involving the practice of magick. A Witch attempts to influence the world around them through the use of the occult. The occult relates to the supernatural and unseen.

Think about it like this: The natural world exists in millions of facets. There are so many ways to engage and connect with the natural world. Our bodies show us several of these ways; we can hear, smell, taste, see, touch, and feel the natural world. This is also true when it comes to connecting with the supernatural world. And the Witch seeks to access and connect with both the natural and the supernatural worlds.

There are countless paths that a Witch might walk. These paths are represented in part by the many traditions of Witchcraft. Each of the different individual traditions represent just one tried and tested way of being a Witch and connecting with magick. One path isn't better than another, but one path may be better for you.

In order to find the path that works for you, you have to experiment, test, try, and connect with different traditions. You might walk down the path of one system of Witchcraft for many years and then be called to another. You might forge your own way, totally eschewing any systems that are already written down. Any entryway to the path of magick is valid and acceptable.

WITCHCRAFT TRADITIONS

There are more traditions of Witchcraft than I could write about in this book, and new traditions are being born every day. There are also hundreds, if not more, of family traditions that you won't and can't have access to— unless it is part of your family lineage and someone teaches you. The only reason I bring up the varying traditions of Witchcraft is because if this is all new for you, it might be easy to assume that there is only one way to do things.

The landscape of modern Witchcraft is a big one, and there are a lot of different ways to be involved. And when you boil it all down, most of the traditions you come across have many of the same early influences. It is what they did with those influences that shifts and changes over time.

Modern Witchcraft really boils down to three paths.

Wicca-Influenced Witchcraft

Wicca was born from Gerald Gardner, who was heavily influenced by occult-ists like Charles Leland, Aleister Crowley, and the Hermetic Order of the Golden Dawn. Initially, Wicca was an initiatory tradition and only those who had been brought into the fold through initiation could practice Wicca.

Over time Wicca became more popular and well known, even a little bit mainstream. Information that was supposed to be oathbound and secret (only available to initiates) became shared outside of those traditions and secret circles. What was once initiatory Wicca started to be written about in books and watered down for a larger audience to access.

Because of this accessibility, there are now tons of variations of Wicca where information is shared without the requirement of initiation. Sometimes non-initiatory Wicca is referred to as *eclectic Wicca*. These are open systems, available to any practitioners. There are many practitioners of Wicca that have never been through an official initiation and that are not connected to any specific Witchcraft lineage.

Specific Wiccan traditions (like Gardnerian Wicca, Alexandrian Wicca, and more) still maintain the lineage of initiation, and these have become known as British Traditional Witchcraft or Wicca (BTW). They have their own specific subset under the umbrella of Wicca.

Virtually all systems with roots in Wicca tend to work with four elements, four directions, casting circles, and drawing down the moon as part of their ritual workings. Most of these systems work with a Goddess and a God. The specifics of these deities will vary depending on tradition or lineage.

Traditionally Influenced Witchcraft

During the occult movement of the 1970s, a branch of Witchcraft practitioners also influenced by occultists from the past came into prominence with a different focus and energy than what the Wiccans were doing. Modern practitioners of this thread of Witchcraft refer to what they do as *Traditional Witchcraft*. Many of these modern practitioners have been heavily influenced by Robert Cochrane and his contemporaries, whose writings were popular in the mid-to-late 1900s. Those practicing Traditional Witchcraft believe that their system of practice is more connected to folklore, specifically from the practices of Western Europe and Britain.

These systems of practice tend to work less with calling the corners, or quarters, and casting circles. The rituals focus more on crossroads and literally drawing out the ritual space on the ground, much like what you might find in Ceremonial magickal systems.

The Traditional Witchcraft groups also work more with Lucifer or the Horned God, with a Goddess varying by specific lineage.

Magickally Influenced Witchcraft

There are all sorts of folks who find Witchcraft because they are seeking magick, spirituality, and power. They don't come through a tradition; they aren't hampered by a structure on how it is supposed to be; they aren't initiated into a system and might not have any sort of formal training.

Witchcraft in this system is anything the practitioners want it to be. It might not fit in any boxes. There is a delicious freedom here, but this thread of Witchcraft can also irritate those who follow a more formal system of practice.

Many folks who practice Witchcraft from this place may not be religious, or they might practice a more mainstream Abrahamic religion. While the other paths of Witchcraft tend to be religious in nature, those who follow a magickally influenced path don't see what they do as religion. Some of these practitioners might not even see what they do as Witchcraft at all.

MAGICK

You've likely noticed that I use the spelling of magick with the *k*. I was taught that magic with a *c* refers to stage or sleight-of-hand magic, while magick with the *k* is the magick that Witches do. Not all Witches follow this spelling protocol, but it is my preference.

Magick is the power that comes *from* ritual, *fuels* ritual, and is expressed *with* ritual. One of the most popular definitions of magick comes from Aleister Crowley: "Magick is the Science and Art of causing Change to occur in Conformity with Will." I prefer Jason Miller's definition of magick, which slightly changes the words: "Magick is the Science and Art of influencing change to occur in conformity to Will."[1] We perform rituals to bring conformity to our will. A ritual is a moment, an opportunity, to align our will with our desires.

Magick is subtle. It's not like the movies, where you speak an incantation and the thing happens right then and there. Magick moves at its own time. It brings forth changes by influencing your thoughts and actions

---

1 Miller, *The Elements of Spellcrafting*, 21.

as well as the thoughts and actions of others. A ritual is the focus of that energy. Performing a ritual gives you the time, space, and opportunity to influence your life toward your desires.

Many people use magick without even realizing it. If you've ever set a goal or made a wish, you've used magick. Sometimes these things will even manifest, but when you incorporate intention, correspondences, and will with your magick, you have a much better shot at seeing your desires come to fruition.

The majority of magick you do won't come in the form of long, drawn-out, formal rituals. Magick happens when you love. Magick sparks when you see something in the world that takes your breath away. Magick is the moment you master a new skill, overcome an obstacle, or feel the fullness of your self-worth. Magick is in the everyday. And so is Witchcraft.

However, when you take time out to perform and connect with ritual, it gives you the opportunity to utilize magick with more awareness and concentration. It is the tool of manipulation for these occult and esoteric forces. Using ritual is like creating a laser focus, bringing all the needed forces into alignment to help you manifest your desires.

UPG

UPG stands for unverified personal gnosis, or historically unexplained, personal esoteric knowledge. This is a fun term that has come into popularity over the last few years. *Gnosis* is a Greek word that means "esoteric knowledge." We each have our own esoteric knowledge that will grow and expand the more we learn and experience. One of the great things about Witchcraft is that we understand your personal spiritual experience is valid and important.

But there may be moments in our studies and rituals that are "unverified," meaning no other Witch or magickal practitioner has shared a similar experience. UPG is great because it gives us permission to have our own personal experiences that don't match what any other person may have written about or shared. However, UPG is also problematic because it allows us to do whatever we want under the protection of saying it is our UPG. This can bring up issues with cultural appropriation, sloppy boundaries, and outright lies.

As with all things, balance is needed. Allow your experiences to be what they are, but don't think that excuses you from learning history and tradition. Having a relationship with both will make you a stronger Witch.

A RITUAL; A SPELL; A MEDITATION

There can be some confusion when we start talking about rituals. The words *ritual*, *spell*, and *meditation* have a lot in common, and this can be confusing for folks who are new to magick and Witchcraft. Some traditions, spiritual practitioners, and individual Witches use these words interchangeably, and that only adds to the confusion. In order to help navigate the potential terminology confusion, here are some key things to know.

Ritual

A ritual encompasses a lot of different things. A ritual can be something you do every day, like taking vitamins. It could also be something you do with reverence or specific directed energy, like a spell or a meditation. Spells and meditations could be included as part of a longer or more complex ritual.

Spell

A spell is, in and of itself, a ritual. In some cases, a spell might require a long, ritualized set up and closing. There may be incantations or chants spoken, and you might feel like you are in a ritual frame of mind. Not all spells can be planned, but that doesn't change the fact that they are rituals.

Some spells are what I refer to as *Emergency Services Magick*. ESM happens when the trouble comes knocking and you need to do spell work right *now*, no time for planning or waiting. With ESM, you might not have time to gather ingredients or cast a circle of protection around your working. The ritualization might be diminished, but it is still a ritual.

Spells are very much rituals, but there are times that the ritual process, the ritual set up, has to fall by the wayside. More on this later.

Meditation

A meditation is also a ritual, like a daily practice, or it might be part of a longer ritual process. It's really common to have a guided meditation, contemplation, or "trance" exercise as a piece of a longer ritual.

And ... ?

Why bring up these terms if they all mean the same thing? Well, here's the rub: there is a bit of paradox because although all of these things are rituals, they also aren't.

A spell is also *not* a ritual. A spell can be a standalone practice. A spell is a focused working where you step in and perform magick and then step out.

A meditation is also *not* a ritual. Meditation is an exercise and a process, but it may not be a ritual in and of itself.

A ritual, a spell, and a meditation are all rituals, and they are all their own things. The difference is how you approach them and your personal spiritual gnosis.

I bring this up merely to point out that your mileage may vary. What you consider a ritual might be a practice that is solely on you. You might hear other practitioners share conflicting information or contradict each other about what rituals look like. The struggle is real, and they are all correct.

When it comes to a magickal practice, our personal tastes, training, and experience will impact how we look at terms and how we implement them into our practices. One size does not fit all.

How to Use This Book: Breath, Bone, and Blood

What awaits you in the following pages are tips, tricks, and guidance for crafting your own rituals. Consider the following steps as a kind of blueprint. What I offer you is the outline and structure of ritual, with plenty of space for your own creative explorations. I will share with you not only the hows of building ritual, but the whys, as well as some historical context. Why do certain things work better than others? How do you even know where to start? Is it possible to get participation from strangers? How do you craft a ritual to perform on your own, with a small group, or with a large group? Read on to find out.

Before we begin, though, I have a few things to mention. Throughout this book, when I refer to the person using ritual technology and tools, I will use the term *Priestex*. This is a genderless term for a ritual leader or facilitator. I will also use the spelling *Godds* to refer to deities; this is a more gender-full spelling to reflect the many emanations of deity. I will also use the words *ritual*, *rite*, and *ceremony* interchangeably. Although these words might have a slightly different meaning, for the purposes of this book, they are all the same.

There is a flow to the sections of this book. This book begins with what I believe to be the building blocks and most important first steps all the way through to the more complicated and less obvious parts of the ritual planning process. My recommendation is to read from beginning to end; the concepts will build on each other.

Throughout the book, there will be text boxes called Home Adventures. These are places where you can practice some of the concepts by creating your own rituals. Try these out in order. Be bold and brave!

There are some exercises and meditations throughout the book. The best way to work with these exercises is to read through them and then record yourself reading them. When you are ready to do the exercise, play the recording so you can fully participate in the process.

It's also important to note that the shape of a ritual can be the same no matter if it is being enacted by a solitary practitioner, a small group like a coven, or a large group. However, the number of ritual participants will change the smaller details and focus of a ritual. Because of that, I will also spend some time discussing how group processes are complicated and how they can be done with ease.

Group process, such as running covens and big public rituals, isn't a topic that has a lot of shared information in the world of Witchcraft. It's not something we talk about all that often, and it has been written about very little. But the way we run our groups is vitally important to the overall health of the Witchcraft world.

For decades (maybe even longer) our groups have practiced in secret. There are lots of reasons for the need for secrecy. However, this secrecy has also allowed for a lot of bad behavior and even abuse. We need to talk about running healthy groups, finding healthy groups, and creating them too!

Even if you are a happy solitary practitioner with no interest in running or joining a group, I highly recommend you read what I've written for covens and groups. You never know when you might be called to leadership. And you never know when another Witch might seek out your wisdom as they search for a group or coven of their own.

This book is divided into three sections: the Breath, the Bone, and the Blood.

THE BREATH

The Breath of Ritual relates to all of the things that go into the initial steps of a ritual coming to life. These are the moments we do every day, the ways we incorporate spiritual practice into our lives. The Breath of Ritual is also the inspiration, the intention, and those very first steps of planning that go into creating a good ritual. It is the Breath of Ritual that makes ritual possible. This is the moment of spark, inspiration, and desire. It's all the steps that happen before we perform any steps of ritual.

THE BONE

The Bones of Ritual are the structures and format of enacting a ritual. It is the process that takes place from set up until the meat of the moment. The Bones of Ritual can often look like the lists, outlines, and written instructions that might be needed to put on a ritual. The Bones of Ritual are the directives and the map that helps us get from one moment to the next. These are the actual steps that need to happen for the ritual to be performed.

THE BLOOD

The Blood of Ritual is the magick and mystery that comes into play with a ritual working. It is the drama, the energy, and the closing up of a ritual. In this section, I will also share ritual pitfalls and problems and how to best avoid them. The Blood of Ritual is what makes it flow. This includes transitions and the things that often go unnoticed when you attend a ritual.

What This Book Is Not

This book is not a guide to transitional moments. This is not a book of rites of passage rituals and honorings. If you'd like to read about rites of passage, check out my book with Gwion Raven, *Life Ritualized*.

This book is also not going to tell you *when* you need to perform a ritual. That is totally your call. It is important that you start to listen to—and trust—your intuition. There is a saying in the Reclaiming tradition of Witchcraft: "You are your own spiritual authority, rooted in community." In order to become your own spiritual authority, you need to have discernment, a relationship with your intuition, and the bravery to take action. That is all up to you, Witch!

SECTION ONE

Breath

The first thing we all do as humans when we arrive earthside is take a breath. Breathing is a magickal act—breath is life. It is a reciprocal action that we take to support all life on the planet. And air is not a renewing resource; all of the air on the planet is all the air that has ever been on the planet. That means the air we breathe is literally the air our ancestors were breathing. How freaking cool is that?

The Breath of Ritual is the air-like influence of the ritual. It is the inspiration, the intention, the spiritual animus in the process. The Breath of Ritual is the first step and it is the last step, much like the breath of life. This is why I say the Breath of Ritual is the most important step of ritual; it is only through awareness of the Breath of Ritual that you will even realize you need to do a ritual or that a ritual is happening.

In this section on the Breath of Ritual, we will go over all the things that happen before the physical action of a rite can take place. We will explore your personal spiritual development, creating intentions, and the things you need to know before you do anything with a ritual.

The Breath of Ritual is a lot of thinking, dreaming, planning, and discussing with other participants and practitioners. The Breath of Ritual must be completed before any of the actual parts of ritual performance can be put together. This part of the planning process is vital to the rest of the planning process. If you try to jump in at another point in the planning, you may find it much harder to focus or create any sort of a plan.

The Breath of Ritual is what makes ritual possible.

Understanding Ritual

If you read through virtually any modern book on Witchcraft and/or Paganism, you will see a rather consistent layout of ritual. That's because most of our modern practices were influenced by the same writers and occultists of the past. Without the influence of groups like the Golden Dawn and individuals like Gerald Gardner, Aleister Crowley, Dion Fortune, and Doreen Valiente, our modern rituals might look very different. Plus, there was hefty borrowing from more mainstream religions.

That's not to say that these common Witchcraft ritual formats are the only ones that exist. No, not by a long shot. There are plenty of other forms, customs, and traditions from folk and Indigenous religious systems, and these practices have also influenced modern Witchcraft. However, we are not talking about Indigenous practices in this book. If you have an interest in any folk or Indigenous ritual format—and you really should, because each one is fascinating and beautiful—I highly encourage you to seek out elders, teachers, and writers from those traditions specifically. Learn from the source.

The wide swath of what we might call Modern Witchcraft is heavily influenced by European folk magick, herb lore, mythology, and the occult. Much of what we take for granted as ritual format is also descended from these systems. Learn this format, practice with it, try it on, and then, if you feel so called, change it. Adjust it to fit your needs and beliefs. After all, this is *your* spiritual practice and *your* spiritual life. It needs to fit you, not the other way around.

Keep in mind, the ritual format that I share in this book is a tried-and-true system. It has been used for decades, if not longer. Think about it like this: The ritual format I am sharing with you is like my family's lasagna recipe. It is really good. It always turns out delicious. And it has been tested for a really long time. Like, this stuff works. But once you totally have the lasagna recipe down and you know it backward and forward, you can try switching it up and add your own style and flair to it. Maybe you want to make a lasagna with a different kind of cheese or in a pot rather than a baking dish. Great! Try that out, but try it once you understand why there is a baking dish and how that impacts the taste. Get my drift?

Many rituals have been written in many books. It's totally okay to read these rituals word for word if you feel called to do so. If you craft your own rituals with the invocations all written out, it is totally okay to memorize these words or to read them off the paper during your ritual. You might also choose not to write out any words for your rituals and just allow the spirit to move through you in the moment. In fact, I highly recommend trying rituals in all of these ways. More on this later on.

RITUAL FLOW

This outline on ritual flow is purely based on the Modern Witchcraft movement. If you were to attend a Witchcraft conference, public ritual, or gathering, it is likely that this format (or something really similar) would be used. This way of performing ritual is only an outline. It gives you the bullet points of ritual, but it is up to you and your creative expression to put flesh on the skeleton.

Here I will go through the ritual steps as bullet points only, but read on. In later sections I will go into more detail and share different ways to perform each of these steps.

Cleansing

Before stepping into ritual space, you should perform a spiritual cleanse. It's simply good spiritual hygiene. If you look at virtually any spiritual practice or religion, there is some form of spiritual cleansing that is done before stepping into a ceremony.

This could come in the form of a literal bath, smoke, drumming or rattling around the physical body, and so much more.

Grounding/Centering

After the spiritual cleanse of your external body comes the internal focusing. Modern life can make us feel pulled in a million different directions, but ritual requires focus and attention on the present moment. Grounding and/or centering will shift your focus from all of the places it doesn't need to be and help you focus on the rite you are stepping into.

Creating the Boundary

Often called *casting the circle* or *creating sacred space*, once you are emotionally, spiritually, and physically ready for the ritual, the next step is to create an energetic boundary between your ritual space and the rest of the world. This is done for two reasons. The first reason is to have a container to hold all of the magick you are doing until you are ready to release it. (Think of it like a cooking pot that holds all your ritual ingredients.) The second reason is to keep out any unwanted energy and influences that aren't needed for your rite. It's a bit of psychic protection and shielding.

Invites

After your boundary is made, the next step is to invite allies and other spiritual powers into your ritual space. These entities are called in as collaborators and witnesses to help the work. In some traditions, this is referred to as an *invocation*, while other traditions use the term *evocation*.

Body

Once you've set up your sacred space, it's time to perform the actual rite. What is the working you are doing? This would be the moment you craft your spell, perform a meditation, or do a reading or oracle working. In later sections I will give you a list of potential things to do as the body of your ritual.

Energy Raising

Ideally after the body piece of the ritual, you move into raising energy. This energy is raised to "feed" the work you've performed, to activate it, and to send your desire/goal out into the world. After the energy raising peaks, there should be a moment of holding to allow the energy to settle or spill out toward your success.

Devoking

Once the energy has settled and it feels like the ritual is complete, it's time to say goodbye to the allies that were invited into the circle. Typically, this is done in reverse order of how they were called into the sacred space. However, there are traditions that devoke allies in the same order they were called in.

Releasing

After allies have been thanked and released from the ritual space, the circle needs to be released too. This is referred to as *opening the circle, closing the circle, releasing the circle*, or *taking the circle down*, depending on the specific tradition of Witchcraft. In some traditions and practices, the circle is released in reverse order of how it was built, and in other traditions it is taken down in the same manner as it was created.

Cleaning Up

This step isn't always necessary, but if you've gathered ritual objects or used any items in your ritual, it is important to clean those pieces up.

Processing

An often-forgotten step of ritual is the decompressing that takes place afterward. It's pretty common to have something important or impactful happen during a ritual. It's a good idea to write this down so you don't lose it. To fully decompress, if you can, use the day after a ritual to relax and review your experience, giving yourself time and space to notice any other feelings that may come up.

Cakes and Ale or Wine

Cakes and ale is the process of grounding after the ritual has been performed or a formal blessing during a ritual. This is traditionally done with a small bit of food, wine, ale, or juice. In some traditions this is done after the energy raising as a way to help your body and spirit ground. In other traditions this is done after the circle has been opened as a way to celebrate the ritual performed, have some community connection time, and, of course, ground. And there are traditions where the cakes and ale part of ritual is connected to the body of the ritual.

EMERGENCY SERVICES MAGICK

There are times when we can't plan a ritual or a spell and won't be able to go through all of the steps listed. There are times when we have to simply jump in and take magickal action. When there's an emergency situation, you won't be able to wait for the perfect moon phase, day of the week, or astrological "moment" to perform your working. In an emergency you don't have time to collect the first rainwater of the season, pick the perfect herb from a sacred site, or gather holey rocks from the beach. You can only act.

In emergencies, you might not be able to gather or use all the tools in your toolbox. You might think this puts you at a disadvantage, and it's true that it is a bit more of an uphill climb, but you have access to that energy in a different form. The energies that come in an emergency situation are fear, adrenaline, and will. You *can* use this to your advantage.

Spells and rituals feed off energy. They need energy in order to be effective, and your will is what directs that energy. Remember earlier, when I said that magick is influencing change to conform with your will? This is what I'm talking about. When it comes to ESM situations, the bonus energy you have access to is adrenaline and, potentially, your fear. If you have a solid relationship with your will, you can utilize these forces.

It's true that you are never without your will, and to cast any spell you must be able to access your willpower. In an emergency, your access to will is the same as it always is, but it is more difficult to control, like a spooked horse. If you have a solid spiritual foundation, you will have better control of your will when fear and adrenaline come into the situation. Having a strong connection to your willpower requires you to have a strong relationship with yourself. This is an area for you to work on before you find yourself in need of ESM.

When you have a solid connection to your will, you can see fear and adrenaline for what they are: emotional and physical reactions. Rather than letting them control you, you can use them as fuel for your magick and spellwork. This isn't something that you can just do in the moment right when it hits the fan. It is something that you need to be practiced at. A relationship with your will won't happen overnight or just fall into place. It takes time and work. It takes having a solid spiritual practice and knowing thyself.

Funnily enough, while working on this book I discovered there is a whole pocket of magickal practitioners that won't do spellwork until they are already in an emergency; they believe magick should only be used for emergency situations. This is not a stance that I agree with, but I do find it very interesting. And your mileage may vary.

THREE KEYS OF WITCHCRAFT

Exploring Witchcraft in any form will bring you into contact with major forces. Some of these will be outside of yourself, but a lot of them will be within you. The most powerful Witches I know have strong and solid relationships with themselves. They have done the "self-work," they know their shadows, and they aren't afraid to face themselves. This is such an important part of Witchcraft. The best way to connect with these parts of yourself and your personal magick are through what I call the Three Keys of Witchcraft: know thyself, discernment, and bravery.

Know Thyself

I talk about this in every class I teach, and I've written about it more times than I can count. One of the most important parts of practicing Witchcraft is developing a better understanding of yourself. What makes you tick and why? How do you relate to the world around you? What resides at the core of you?

If you don't seek out the answers to these questions when you start on the path of Witchcraft, you will quickly find that you are confronted with the things that force you to look for the answers.

Knowing and understanding yourself will bring you more power than any ritual or spell ever could. It is the true practice of the Witch.

Discernment

You might think the Witch's most important tool is their wand, or that their most potent forces are their chants or spells, but none of that is true. The most powerful thing a Witch has at their disposal is their discernment.

Discernment is literally the ability to judge well. This might sound easy, but it's a skill that takes time to develop.

Many practitioners new to Witchcraft, spells, and ritual are worried and afraid to do anything "wrong." They don't want to cause harm, piss off deities, or make their ancestors mad. New practitioners don't want to call down fire and brimstone from the heavens, have unexpected negative consequences, or make a serious spiritual blunder. Of course, I totally get it. No one wants to make a spiritual ass out of themselves.

This is where discernment comes in. You must be able to judge well.

Witchcraft and magick have been written about for thousands of years. It won't take you long to read contradictory information about magickal forces and how to do things the "right" way, even though that "right" way is the exact opposite of what some other person said. How do we know what is "right"?

You can't take anything in life at face value, and you need to run anything and everything through your own set of beliefs, values, and practices. If something doesn't smell right, leave it alone. If you don't feel safe with a practice, don't do it. If you are uncertain, ask more experienced folks for help or set it aside and come back to it at a later date.

The most important spiritual relationship you have is with yourself. Know your inner voice. Know your intuition. Know your discernment.

Bravery

The other side of discernment is bravery. If we get caught up in reading, studying, watching, learning, and trying to suss out the best plan of action, we might not ever *take* action.

I teach Witchcraft classes to a lot of new practitioners. Witches who are new to the practice and looking for help finding their path are often afraid of making mistakes. For some new Witches, this is such a big fear that they stop exploring the path altogether.

Witchcraft requires bravery. For hundreds of years, and in some parts of the world even now, being accused of Witchcraft could get you killed. It is an act of rebellion and kicking sand in the face of the overculture to call yourself a Witch. You can't do any of that if you're not brave.

And by the way, bravery isn't something you are. It is something you *choose*. Fear keeps us stuck, but we can look down at fear and overcome it. We can choose bravery. I encourage you to choose bravery.

Living a Spiritual Life

Rituals can be a part of your life when you fancy it, on a whim, or after weeks of planning. You can participate in rituals whenever you feel the call. However, your rituals will be more effective and powerful if you have a strong spiritual practice that you can base them off of.

I brought this up with the Three Keys of Witchcraft. I believe the words *know thyself* are the most important of all spiritual tenets. These words were written above the doors of the Oracle at Delphi. These words have inspired many spiritual teachers and leaders. And the work of knowing thyself never ends.

As a spiritual practitioner, you need to understand your strengths and growing edges. In order to be a better, stronger human, you need to know what triggers you and why. Walking a spiritual path is one fraught with unknown shadows, challenges, and fears. Practicing Witchcraft will put you in front of all the things that make you quake in your boots. If you aren't mentally, emotionally, and spiritually prepared for facing those things, you are in for trouble.

Figuring out your triggers, challenges, and growing edges can't be done by reading a single book, attending one workshop, or journaling a few times. This is the work of your life. Throughout this book, and throughout your spiritual life, you will return again and again to the practice of knowing thyself.

GROWING EDGES

What is a growing edge, you ask? Great question!

A growing edge is something that you might consider a "weakness." You know when you go into a job interview and they ask you to name one of your strengths and one of your weaknesses? It's similar to that. Except it is more than that.

In the overculture, a weakness is looked at as a negative thing. A weakness is a part of yourself that you have deemed not good enough. It is a thing that holds you back. However, there is no weakness that you can't work with, embrace, change, or become friends with.

For example, once upon a time I would have said that I had a weakness as a Priestex. I was terrified to sing in public. I don't mean I was terrified to sing in front of people—I mean I was vomit-inducingly scared to even sing with other people in the same room as me. As a Priestex in the Reclaiming tradition, singing is something we do at practically every ritual. No one is ever forced or expected to do something they aren't comfortable with, but it was embarrassing to me that I couldn't even whisper the words to songs or chants in front of, or with, other people. I wanted to change this thing I had deemed a weakness.

The first step was to shift my perspective. Instead of seeing not being able to sing as a weakness, I started to see it as a growing edge. Singing was a skill that I didn't yet possess, but I wanted to. It was a thing that terrified me, but I wanted to overcome it.

Once I shifted from looking at singing as a weakness to a growing edge, I started to give myself permission to push that edge, carefully and slowly. First, I encouraged myself to whisper the words of songs during rituals. I had always mouthed the words before that, so no one would know I wasn't singing along. But I pushed the edge to make a noise.

When that started to feel more comfortable, I pushed the edge a little bit more. I allowed myself to sing out loud with other people during public rituals. I convinced myself that no one was even listening to me. There were a hundred other voices singing and there was no way anyone would even hear my voice among all the other people singing. Totally doable.

After this shift, I broke through the first level of fear. I was able to sing during public rituals, but only when other people were singing. As I started to Priestex in public rituals more and more, it became clear to me that I wanted to push that growing edge even further. I wanted to be able to sing solo in front of other people.

And so, I decided to volunteer to teach the song we would be using for the public summer solstice ritual that I was helping plan. Right before the ritual started, I was terrified. I was literally shaking and nauseous. I was *so* scared. But I stepped forward at the beginning of the ritual and sang in front of all the people in attendance.

I think I blacked out because I remember none of it. But I know that I did it! I didn't die, no one laughed at me, and no one threw rotten vegetables at me. I wasn't kicked out of the ritual. I did it!

Since then, I've taught songs at many public rituals. I've even sung on my own during classes. I'm not scared anymore. When I think about singing now, it feels like no big deal. But the me of ten years ago would have vomited at the thought of what comes so easily now.

I faced a weakness in my practice and I turned it into a growing edge. After pushing that growing edge, I turned it into a strength. This is part of knowing thyself. This is part of Witchcraft and what it means to be a Witch.

SAYING THE WORDS

I've talked with a lot of new practitioners that either don't feel like they have the authority to say the words written in a ritual or feel silly saying the words out loud.

My first reaction to this is *you must say the words*. In fact, you must say the words of a ritual out loud. If you feel silly, good! Do it anyway. Eventually you won't feel silly anymore. There is power in spoken words. Saying something out loud gives it power, so much more power than if you only say it in your head.

When you speak, your voice creates vibration, and that vibration feeds the energy of your words. Words have power. So, speak your rituals out loud. If the words written by someone else don't feel right or you don't feel like you have the proper authority to speak them, then read them over, understand what they mean, and use your own words instead.

In some traditions, there is an expectation that you will memorize the traditional written rituals, and there is specific liturgy for almost any ritual you could want to perform. In other traditions, there is specific liturgy but it is totally okay for you to read from a script rather than memorize it. And then there are traditions where there is no expectation to even have written rituals; you just allow spirit to speak through you. But in all of these systems, there is an expectation that you will speak out loud.

There are practitioners out there who never speak the words of ritual out loud and don't encourage or ask their coveners or students to do it either. This is a major disservice to magick. If you can't even speak the words out loud, are you sure you're really ready to perform magick? Are you sure you're really ready to be a Witch?

Once I was a member of a fledgling Grove in a Druid organization. This group was made up of me, my partner, and my best friend—the two people I knew and trusted most in the world. One of our first lessons together was to do a series of physical gestures and make a series of corresponding tones. It was awkward.

Even though I was close with, and trusted, these two people, making weird "woo-woo" noises together was super uncomfortable. We giggled a lot that first go around. We were all rather shocked that it was so difficult for us to go through this process together. It took a significant amount of time to stop the giggles and shift into a deeper focus. When we finally got there, it was a transformative moment. We all had a similar reaction and felt excited to continue the practice together.

If we had allowed ourselves to imagine, visualize, or just do the toning "in our heads," we would have been missing out on the real part of this practice. Creating sound is creating power.

LAW OF ATTRACTION

The concept of the Law of Attraction (LoA) has made its way into modern Witchcraft, which is a bit problematic if you ask me. The Law of Attraction is a concept that states we create and manifest what we desire: if we focus our thoughts on the positive, that is what we will get, and if we focus on the negative, that's what we get. But the LoA has been oversimplified and watered down for a more mainstream audience.

The truth is, if you see nothing but negativity in the world, you are a lot more likely to have that bias confirmed over and over again. Bad things will continually happen, and they will all reinforce your belief that the world sucks. When good things happen, they will be overshadowed by the troubles.

If you see nothing but positivity in the world, you are a lot more likely to have that bias confirmed. When good things happen, it will reinforce your belief that the world is good. And when bad things happen, you will be more likely to find the silver lining or see how it was a blessing in disguise.

However, most people can't hold a purely negative or positive relationship with the world. We are not black and white, but a rainbow of complexity.

Another issue with the oversimplification of the LoA—and I cannot stress this enough—is this idea that when bad things happen in our lives, it is because we brought it on ourselves due to our negative thinking. *You don't cause trauma or abuse in your life.* Bad things happen because bad things happen; it is a part of life. It is how we deal with these things that changes.

Shifting our thoughts to focus on what we want to create in our lives helps us see potential and possibility. Staying in a positive mindset helps pull us out of depression and struggle. However, it doesn't mean that we will never struggle, fall into depression, or have hardships. And sometimes all of the positive thinking in the world won't change circumstances that are beyond our control.

Ultimately, you are only in control of your mindset. Does that mean it is always easy? No. Does that mean you won't struggle? No. Does that mean you don't need to take medication or get therapy when you are in a bad mental state? No.

The Law of Attraction is important when it comes to our rituals and spellwork. If we doubt ourselves and don't believe in our magick or power, we are doomed to fail.

SPIRITUAL PRACTICE

Having a strong and solid daily practice is an important part of living a spiritual life. Working on yourself is an important part of being a Witch. Are these things specifically related to crafting powerful rituals? Well, yes and no.

When I say no, I mean you can perform a ritual with no awareness of what you're doing. You could cast a spell having never learned anything about Witchcraft, simply out of sheer desperation. It happens all the time. These spells may or may not be successful, but if you want long-term success, consistent success, and faster success with your magick, you are better served by having strong spiritual muscles.

When I say yes, I mean that having a spiritual life, having a daily practice, and working on yourself will help your rituals be stronger and more impactful because your spiritual body will be stronger and therefore have a bigger impact.

Think of your spiritual practice as the foundation of a house—*your* house, you. Before you can create the rooms where you will live, celebrate, and spend your time, you have to have a strong, solid, and well-built foundation. A spiritual practice helps create that foundation.

What does that mean? What's a spiritual practice? Simply put, a spiritual practice is a regular set of actions that connect you to something bigger than yourself. This could come through several different experiences, but the most important word here is *regular*. Your spiritual work can't happen occasionally or sporadically. It needs to be done on the regular, think daily, in order for it to have the most impact on your life.

So, what makes up a spiritual practice?

- **Meditation:** Meditation is a process of quieting the mind, going within, and allowing yourself to be present. There are dozens of different ways to meditate.
- **Breathwork:** Breathwork can calm you, shift your awareness, and bring elation. Just like meditation, there are many different ways to do breathwork.

- **Therapy:** This might not be a daily practice, but getting professional help to deal with and process your trauma is an important part of growing your spiritual strength.
- **Journaling:** Write a few pages a day. It doesn't have to be on any particular subject; just allow your thoughts to flow out of your head. You can do this with paper and pen, on your phone, or on a computer.
- **Divination:** Pulling a tarot card or rune, or using another form of divination, can help you step into the flow of your intuition, which is a powerful part of your spiritual life.
- **Chanting:** The repetition of a chant or mantra can help shift your awareness and bring a sense of calm. There are lots of different chants that can be used, but the best ones are simple and short.
- **Singing:** Much like chanting, singing for an extended period of time calms the mind and shifts awareness. Songs that are uplifting or spiritual in nature are best.
- **Dancing:** Physical movement is good spiritual work. Our minds, bodies, and spirits all need connection, to each other and to divinity. Dance to music that is uplifting or spiritual in nature.
- **Exercise:** Spiritual work isn't just silence or stillness—it can also be movement and improving your physical strength. That doesn't mean you have to pump iron at the gym, but physical exercise that is appropriate for your body is a good place to start.
- **Affirmations:** Writing out a positive affirmation as a blessing for yourself is powerful magick. Place this affirmation somewhere you will see it every day, like your bathroom mirror. Speak it out loud every time you see it.
- **Spellwork:** Performing magick on the regular will connect you to something bigger than yourself and helps provide information about your inner spiritual workings.
- **Ritual:** Yes, ritual.

✦ *Home Adventures* ✦

Now it's time for you to explore daily practice. Look at the list of potential daily practices and pick out two to try out. Remember, it takes two to three weeks to develop a new habit, but only two days to break that habit. Dedicate at least two weeks to any of these practices. Take notes as you try out these things in order to track how successful the different practices might be for you.

When You Decide to Perform a Ritual

Sometimes you need to do a little work ahead of time to determine what the best course of action might be. There are ways to begin to step into the ritual flow before taking on any of the ritual planning steps. What I am talking about here isn't just the steps for getting ready for ritual, but the steps for getting ready to get ready for ritual.

Before planning or performing a ceremony, you might want some guidance or clarity. You might not be totally certain what kind of rite to perform or what the best direction or timing might be. A ritual can change you, your life, your circumstances—you might think you are ready for that, but the reality of these changes might take you by surprise. Being prepared will help.

EMOTIONAL PREP

Your mind and emotions might feel ready for change, but when that change comes, you will need to face the new reality of your situation. In some instances, change might feel like a relief or an increase in personal power. In others instances, change might feel jarring or even shocking.

One way to start to prepare for this is to begin to visualize what your life could look like after the shift. See yourself having manifested your desire. See yourself with a stronger relationship to a deity. See yourself with a deeper understanding of your place in the world. What might your life look/feel/be like after the ritual is completed?

I would highly encourage you to write these things down. Keep track of your feelings and desires pre-ritual. After the ritual is complete, look back at what you have written and see how it resonates with you.

SPIRITUAL PREP

Spiritually, you won't really have much of an idea how things could be different after you perform your ritual. Things will shift on a level that you might not even be aware of until much later. However, there are still ways you can prepare for some of the spiritual shifts that might occur.

Meditating on your goal ahead of time can help to bring a sense of awareness and calm to your process. Taking time out for calming, grounding, and centering before a ritual will help you step into a magickal state more easily. Taking time out for calming, grounding, and centering after a ritual will help you integrate your experience more easily.

MUNDANE PREP

A little research goes a long way. As you prepare yourself in all the ways that you can, you should also do a little real-world searching. Have rituals like this one been done before? How have others gone about performing these rites? Is there some historical context related to what you want to create?

Remember your Witch's tool of discernment. Do some reading in books and online to see what sort of ritual inspiration comes forward for your working. Write down any notes, ideas, keywords, or concepts that you discover.

DIVINATION

Performing divination before starting any ritual planning can help provide clarity on the best course of action and give you details about what kind of rite to perform. Divination is simply a tool for engaging with your own intuition. It comes in many forms: tarot cards, oracle cards, runes, ogham, shells, bone sets, scrying, dice, bibliomancy, and more. If you already perform divination, you can use any system you enjoy. If this is new to you, consider seeking out a professional reader to help you.

I also use tarot as a form of divination to help me determine what type of spellwork or ritual might best serve the situation. This system is based on the suits of the tarot, so it uses only the minor arcana. I take the minor arcana out of the deck and pull one to three cards. The suits that show up in the reading help me determine what course of action my ritual should take.

- **Swords:** Perform a ritual involving music, singing, spoken word, incense, or smoke.
- **Wands:** Perform a ritual that involves burning items to release, burning herbs, or candle magick.
- **Cups:** Perform a ritual that involves bathing, water, or asperging of some form.
- **Pentacles:** Perform a ritual involving offerings, tangible items that you can carry on your person, soil, salt, or food.

✦ Home Adventures ✦

Now that you have read some of the ways to prepare for crafting a ritual, perform some of these steps in preparation for your own ritual. You might not know what that ritual is yet, or you might have a really clear idea of the ritual you need or want to create. Either way, start here and do some searching.

- Perform divination on the best course of action for your current situation or desire.
- Journal about how you could emotionally and spiritually prepare for this rite. What shifts do you imagine might come from this process?
- Do some research and get a handful of ideas for how you might enact your ritual.

Inspiration: Where Do Rituals Come From?

Crafting a ritual is a lot like painting a picture. It is art. We don't really understand where art comes from. The ancient Greeks had the Muses, divine beings that brought forth specific arts and talents. The ancient Celts had Awen, the spirit of inspiration that any person could access; it bestowed skill and talent. Psychology has the collective unconscious, that ethereal place where all beauty and art connects us.

No matter where art comes from, the clear message is that we all have access to it. The same is true for rituals.

Ritual is a product of desire. It might be a desire to shift your reality through the use of a spell. It could be a desire to celebrate the turning of the Wheel and seasonal shifts. Perhaps it is the desire to commune with a deity or nature spirit. No matter what, desire is the starting point.

Once desire has sparked, we have to be quiet and listen. Rituals can play out in hundreds of different ways. In order to determine the best way to direct your desire, you have to shape how to best let that desire unfold.

Some of the places we can find inspiration are laid out in the book *Witch's Wheel of the Year* by Jason Mankey. He writes about how every ritual is different, but there are six main areas of focus (or inspiration) for ritual. He names these areas as:

- **The Natural World:** Rituals where we connect with nature and/ or nature spirits. These may also look like ritual where we offer magick to heal the land or waters.
- **Seasons and the Wheel of the Year:** Rituals where we connect with the changing of the seasons and the religious and secular holidays that happen as the Wheel turns.
- **Magick:** Rituals where we perform spells.
- **Deity and Other Higher Powers:** Rituals where we connect with higher powers in the form of deities. These may come in the form of devotion or in celebration and communion.

- **Ancestors, Spirit Animals, and the Fey:** Rituals where we connect with higher powers in the forms of land spirits, nature spirits, ancestors, or animal guides.
- **Community:** Rituals that make space for a group to bond and connect. These types of rituals are especially important for covens and small groups that will work magick together.[2]

In the book *Life Ritualized*, Gwion Raven and I write about the beginning of a rite of passage coming from a catalyst.[3] Sometimes that catalyst comes from outside forces, and sometimes that catalyst comes from an inner yearning for change. Although this concept is focused more on specific rituals for rites of passage, the catalyst for ritual applies to any form of ritual.

When it comes to rituals, a catalyst might come in the form of wanting to honor the turning of the Wheel. This could also show up with a desire for a change of circumstances and crafting a spell to improve a part of your life. The catalyst could be seasonal, religious, or a myriad of other things.

Ultimately, the catalyst is a spiritual desire to serve, or change, or connect. It is a calling to step into the magickal realms for yourself, your loved ones, your spiritual guides and allies, or your community.

Crafting Intentions: Why Are We Doing This?

After the initial spark of desire, the next step is to determine the *why* of the situation. Why are you going to take action on that desire? What do you hope to gain from performing the ritual? Do you want this ritual to bring world peace? Do you want this ritual to bring you a windfall of cash? Do you want this ritual to prove to your Goddess that you adore her? The *why* of the ritual adds the first layer of form to what you are going to do. It gives your rite a focus. It is from that place of desire, and it is why we craft an intention.

A ritual intention is literally a sentence or two on what it is you are doing. Writing out your ritual intention brings clarity to the work at hand.

---

2   Mankey, *Witch's Wheel of the Year*, 8–11.

3   LeFae and Raven, *Life Ritualized*, 25.

An intention is a powerful tool. If at any point in your ritual-planning process you find yourself stuck or confused, simply go back to the *why*—go back to your intention. Remembering why you are performing a ritual will help you keep on track throughout the planning process.

However, a word of warning: there is a slight danger in writing out your intentions. You might feel compelled to include every buzzword, desire, and all the flowery language you know into one intention. Your first draft intention might end up being a full page of words. Trust me, that's too many words. Your intention needs to encapsulate the point of the ceremony. It needs to get to the heart of what you want to do. Say it in as few words as possible.

A ritual intention needs to sum up the goal of your rite in one to three sentences. It needs to represent the essence of what you are doing. It is not a laundry list of every step you plan to take along the way.

Depending on your personal proclivities, you might also want to make your ritual intentions flowery and poetic. Of course, that is okay, but don't let your desire to be poetic take away from keeping your intention to a couple of short sentences. The best thing to remember when crafting an intention is to keep it simple and easy; this advice will serve you throughout the rest of the ritual planning process.

It's also important to be careful what you wish for in regard to your ritual intention. When doing a spell or transformational ritual, you need to be clear on your intention and what you are calling in while also leaving room for mystery. Sometimes our desire on the surface isn't actually what we need from our spell or ritual.

For example, if you decide to do a ritual for money and you want to cast a spell to call in one thousand dollars, that's great and it points to a clear desire for money, but what is the underlying issue? What brought you to the point of needing $1,000 in a hurry? Is it that you need a better-paying job? Is it that you need a roommate to help cover monthly expenses? Is it that you need to pay off debt? Was this just a random financial emergency? Look at the underlying issues and work your rites from *that* place rather than from the surface.

Here are some intention examples to help get your ritual juices flowing:

- **Devotional Ritual Intention Example:** I will call upon Aphrodite to seek her wisdom of self-love and shower her with devotions.
- **Spell Ritual Intention Example:** I will raise energy for the success of my new business venture.
- **Seasonal Ritual Intention Example:** We will honor the turning of the Wheel by dancing the Maypole in celebration of community.

PLANNING INTENTIONS: WHAT ARE WE DOING?

Once you have a solid idea of why you are planning to perform a ritual, the next step is to plan the outline of said ritual. It is the *what* of the process. All rituals follow a format of sorts; we've already gone over that, and in the next section we will go more deeply into that format.

Having a clear and concise intention will help the "what are we doing?" part of the ritual planning come together more easily. And in some cases, the intention will fill out some of that ritual outline. For example, in the Seasonal Ritual Intention Example, the ritual intention mentions dancing the Maypole and the celebration of community. It would make sense for this ritual to have a Maypole dance and some sort of group celebration.

With the intention crafted, part of the ritual planning process is already completed.

✦ Home Adventures ✦

It's time for you to craft your own intention! Whether this is the first time you've ever crafted an intention or it is old hat, we are going to practice our intention-making skills.

To start, ground yourself, come to a place of centeredness, and give yourself some time to contemplate. Go within and ponder what kind of rite might serve you right now. What would be good for you to ritualize? Perhaps you need a long spiritual cleanse. Perhaps you want to cast a protection spell. Perhaps you need to honor a specific rite of passage you are experiencing. Any choice is the right choice.

Once you have a clear idea of what you want to create a ritual for, write this down, and write down all your thoughts on the subject. What you write might be a whole page or a paragraph. Any length is fine; allow all the words that need to be said to be written out.

When that is done, look over what you have written and fine-tune your words. Narrow your writing down to the essence of what you want your ritual to be. Ideally, this will narrow your words down to no more than three sentences.

Practical Considerations

In the early planning stages of a ritual, there are some things that should be taken into consideration. This will cover some practical points that can really help the early stages of ritual planning be smooth, from working with correspondences to some of the more subtle nuances of getting into the ritual-planning process.

RITUAL PARTICIPANTS

One of the first things to take into consideration in your planning is to look at who your ritual is for. Is this a ritual just for you? Is this a ritual for your small coven or group? Is this a ritual for a large public event?

And who are the people that make up that contingent? Are there folks with mobility issues that you need to make sure are taken into consideration? Will there be participants that can't stand for long periods of time or won't be able to sit on the ground? Is it possible there will be participants with small children in tow? And if so, will you have activities to keep kids engaged, either as part of the ritual or as an offshoot?

Knowing who will likely be at your ritual will help you determine how to best set up your ritual.

RITUAL PREP

Leading up to the ritual, it is a good idea to practice. This will help you find areas where there may be holes, kinks, or problems in the ritual format. A rehearsal can help you smooth out any issues that may have been overlooked during the ritual planning. If you are writing out a ritual, it is also good to practice and see how memorization might be coming along.

RITUAL LOCATION

Yes, location makes all the difference. If you are planning a ritual for a public park, you need to make sure you have a plan for bad weather. If you are planning a ritual for a hotel room, you need to have a plan for dealing with the sterility of the space. If you are planning a ritual for your own home, how will you move or adjust your belongings to make the space work?

Also, remember it always goes back to your ritual intention. If your ritual purpose is to connect with the wild spirits of a specific forest, perhaps you want to hold your ritual in said forest. However, if you have ritual participants with mobility issues and there are no paved trails to your spot in the forest, you might need to make another plan.

When determining the location of a ritual, also take into consideration what you can do to that space. If you are planning a ritual in a hotel room where you can't hang lights or put anything up on the walls, you might need to really think if that is the best space. Are there other creative changes you can make?

RITUAL SUPPLIES

Once you have a clear intention and you know what form your ritual will take, you need to consider what supplies are necessary to make the ritual happen. All rituals have supplies. There's nothing worse than being in the middle of a rite and then realizing there is an important component you need that you don't have. Some supplies will be obvious, like your ritual tools, for example. Or if your ritual is to perform a Maypole dance, you'll need a pole and ribbons.

But some supplies might take a little more research and planning. It's a good idea to go through your ritual outline piece by piece and write down any materials or supplies that will be needed for all the parts of the ceremony.

Here are some ritual supplies you might want to add to your list:

- **Altar Decorations:** Flowers, bowls, or decorations to add to the ambiance of the ritual.
- **Candles:** May or may not be needed. Many rental halls for larger rituals won't allow fire in any form. LED or battery-operated candles will work as a replacement. However, if you are doing candle spellwork, make sure you have the appropriate candles in the appropriate colors ready to go.
- **Cash Box and Change, if Charging Admittance:** For larger public rituals.
- **Drums or Other Musical Supplies:** This includes electronic devices if you will be using recorded music in your ritual.
- **Fire-Making Supplies, Like Matches or a Lighter:** An often-forgotten tool! Make sure you have what you need to create fire if that is part of the ritual.
- **Herbs:** May be needed for spellwork. You will need to research what herbs you want to have available prior to the ritual.
- **Incense and Incense Burners:** Again, many rental halls for larger rituals won't allow for incense burning. Plus, many people have scent sensitivities. Typically, incense is left out of big public rituals, but for smaller gatherings or solitary rituals, have your incense already in a burner before starting your ritual.
- **Infrastructure, Like Tables, Chairs, Cushions, etc.:** Larger halls for big rituals will often provide these things, but make sure you know before setting up for the ceremony. If you need participants to bring their own, that will need to be announced ahead of time.
- **Lighting:** The lighting of a ritual can make or break the atmosphere. Bring what you need with you.
- **Magickal Supplies:** There may be dirt, washes, waters, tarot cards, ribbons, or other forms of magickal supplies needed.
- **Offerings:** Have food and drink ready to go before the ritual begins.

- **Practical Supplies:** You may need paper, pens, name tags, water cups, plates for food, baskets for offerings, and more for your ritual. Make sure you have these ready to go ahead of time.
- **Ritual Tools:** An athame, broom, chalice, cauldron, mirror, pentacle, wand, etc. Grab what you will need for the working and have it on the altar before beginning.
- **Signage for What Event Is Happening:** Sandwich boards, A-frame signs, posters, and so on will help folks attending a public ritual know that they are in the right place.
- **Stones:** May be needed for spellwork or other magickal practices. You will need to research what stones you want to have available prior to the ritual.
- **Table Coverings or Altar Cloths:** These could be considered altar decorations, but they have their own bullet point because you might have other tables that need covering besides the main altar.

RITUAL ETIQUETTE

When attending a ritual, there are some basic forms of etiquette that should be paid attention to. This is very similar to the idea of table manners when going over to another person's home for a meal. Some families (Witchcraft traditions) will have very strict rules about where the silverware (ritual tools) goes or the use of cloth napkins (ritual attire) or in what order to eat things (the layout of the ritual), while other families are more freeform and don't worry too much about structure.

It's good spiritual manners to get the general layout of the land before going into a ritual. If you've been invited, ask the person who invited you what to expect. If you are attending a larger public function, there is often a welcome that happens at the beginning of the gathering where many of these concepts will be covered. However, there are a few pieces of ritual etiquette that are pretty universal with most traditions and systems of practice:

- Don't touch someone else's ritual tools or objects on an altar unless you have been given explicit permission.

- You may need to energetically "cut" yourself out of the ritual space in order to help hold the integrity of the ritual container.
- It is best to not interrupt Priestexes when they are speaking. However, if you can't hear them, you can shout out "Say it friend" as a way to let them know you can't hear what they are saying.
- If you are asked to sing, sing. If you are asked to dance, dance to a level you are able. If you are asked to move to a different place, move as best as you can.
- If you feel uncertain, watch the level that other participants participate at in order to give you a good gauge of what is expected.

Magickal Timing

Having the right timing for a spell means that you have divine power on your side. Paying attention to timing, astrological events, days of the week, and more can have an impact on your rituals. Using the right timing can help make your rites and rituals easier and add energy to any work that you are doing.

DAYS OF THE WEEK

Here's the funny thing: our current calendar and system for tracking time isn't really that old. The Gregorian calendar came into existence in 1582 when Pope Gregory XIII reformed the calendar for the Catholic church. This impacted Italy, Portugal, Spain, and some of Germany. By 1699 the rest of Germany switched to this calendar. Other parts of the world adopted the new calendar later: Britain and the colonies switched over in 1752, Sweden in 1753, Japan in 1873, China in 1912, the Soviet Union in 1918, and Greece in 1923.[4]

But the way we split up time doesn't just come from Pope Gregory XIII. The concept of seven days of the week originates from the ancient Babylonians, who split the week into seven days based on the seven planets in

---

4   The Editors of Encyclopaedia Britannica, "Gregorian calendar," *Encyclopaedia Britannica*, last modified April 19, 2021, https://www.britannica.com/topic/Gregorian-calendar.

their astrological system. They also gave every hour of the day a planetary correspondence.[5]

Later, the ancient Greeks changed the names of the days of the week to match their Gods. And then the Romans replaced the Greek Gods with their Roman counterparts. Then, sometime in the fourth century, the Anglo-Saxons replaced the Roman Gods with the names of their deities. The English words for days of the week are more closely aligned with the Anglo-Saxon names, while French and Spanish match the Roman names more closely.[6]

- **Monday:** Named for the planetary body the moon. Some relate Mondays to the Goddesses Hecate and Selene. This day of the week is good for magick relating to dreams, clairvoyance, protection, and healing. This is also a good day for keeping spellwork hidden or revealing secrets.
- **Tuesday:** Named for the planet Mars and the Anglo-Saxon God Tyr. This day of the week is good for magick relating to aggression, passion, and justice. This is also a good day for spells related to battle, action, and honor.
- **Wednesday:** Named for the planet Mercury and the Anglo-Saxon God Odin. This day of the week is good for magick relating to cleverness, travel, wisdom, and money. This is also a good day for spells related to sorting out money issues, improving skills, and divination.
- **Thursday:** Named for the planet Jupiter and the Anglo-Saxon God Thor. This day of the week is good for abundance, prosperity, success, and honor. This is also a good day for spells related to luck, money, and desire.
- **Friday:** Named for the planet Venus and the Anglo-Saxon God Freya. This day of the week is good for love, sex, beauty, and happiness. This is also a good day for spells related to relationships, pleasure, and general magick.

---

5   Coolman, "Origins of the Days of the Week."
6   Coolman, "Origins of the Days of the Week."

- **Saturday:** Named for the planet Saturn. Some relate Saturday to the Goddess Hecate and the God Saturn. This day of the week is good for money, business, and boundaries. This is also a good day for spells relating to clearing obstacles, protection, banishment, and wisdom.
- **Sunday:** Named for the planetary body the sun. Some relate Sunday to the Goddess Brigid and the Titan Helios. This day of the week is good for justice, leadership, hope, and success. This is also a good day for spells related to goals, healing, divination, and prosperity.[7]

TIME OF THE DAY

Each day can be broken into four different segments of time. Each of these segments of time have different energetic signatures that can help influence your magick and rituals.

- **Dawn:** The energy of dawn is connected to the element of air, the sword and the athame, and the east. It is the power of Venus and the archangel Raphael. The magick of dawn is for activation and beginnings. It is the magick of hope, vitality, and releasing.
- **Midday:** The energy of midday is connected to the element of fire, wands, and the south. It is the power of the sun and the archangel Michael. The magick of midday is for power, strength, and focus.
- **Dusk:** The energy of dusk is connected to the element of water, chalices, and the west. It is the power of Venus and the archangel Gabriel. The magick of dusk is for banishing, releasing, grief, and connection to the Otherworlds.
- **Midnight:** The energy of midnight is connected to the element of earth, pentacles, and the north. It is the power of the planet Earth and the archangel Uriel. The magick of midnight is for all magick, releasing, grounding, and cursing.

---

7 Kynes, *Llewellyn's Complete Book of Correspondences*, 391–93.

CLOCK HANDS

We've lost a lot of the magick of the clock now that most folks use a digital clock. But magickally, the movement of the hands of a clock could be incorporated into rituals and spells. This isn't about the specific "time," but rather the directions the hands are moving. Bonus points when you incorporate planetary hours into the mix.

Working with the hands of the clock for your rituals is really very simple. When both the hands are moving upward, this is the time to do magick for calling in your desires. When both the hands are moving downward, this is the time to do magick for releasing and banishing.

MOON PHASES

Everyone knows that Witches work with the power of the moon for spells and ceremonies, right? The moon is the heavenly body that is closest to us. It has been a friend and ally since the dawn of time. People have been entranced by the moon for as long as we have been around.

The power the moon has on our planet can literally be seen and measured. The pull of the moon creates waves in our oceans. The rising and falling of the tides is due to the moon. If the moon can make tides and oceans have waves, it just makes sense that this powerful force would also impact our human bodies and our magick.

- Full Moon: The power of the moon is at its peak at this time. The full moon holds the power of abundance and illumination. It is a good time to perform magick for activation and manifestation as well as divination, casting spells, or doing general magick for increasing and calling in. The full moons throughout the year will each have a different energetic focus. The energy of the full moon typically lasts for about three days.
- Waning Moon: The power of the moon is in its decline at this time. The waning moon holds the power of decrease and clearing. It is a good time to perform magick for banishing, reversal spells, and rituals for personal transformation, as well as rituals for loss

and clearing grief. The waning moon goes from waning gibbous (almost full) to waning crescent (almost dark), with the moon appearing smaller and smaller as it goes.

- **Dark Moon:** The phrases dark moon and new moon are often used interchangeably, but they are two different moments in the moon's cycle. The dark moon is the moment where there appears to be no moon in the sky. This could last for a few seconds to several days, depending on the other astrological events happening at the time. The dark moon holds the power of secrets and hidden things. It is a good time to perform magick you want to keep secret and unseen.
- **New Moon:** The new moon is the first sliver of light in the sky after the dark moon phase has completed. The new moon holds the power of beginnings, intentions, and divination. It is a good time to work magick for what you want to create and build in the coming weeks.
- **Waxing Moon:** The power of the moon is increasing at this time. The waxing moon holds the power of increase and growth. It is a good time to perform magick for abundance, creativity, inspiration, and motivation, as well as rituals for growth and power. The waxing moon goes from waxing crescent (almost new) to waxing gibbous (almost full), the moon appearing larger and larger as it goes.

PLANETS

Using planetary influences with ritual can stem from an interest in astrology or just wanting to understand how the different planets' energies can help or hinder your spellcrafting and ceremonies.

Astrology is a whole system that can be studied and incorporated into your rituals. Using astrology, you can determine specific times that are the most in alignment with the ritual you want to perform.

Earth: The planet we live on. Earth is connected to the astrological signs of Taurus, Virgo, and Capricorn. It rules midnight and the season of winter. Earth magick is good for real-world issues, grounding, and protection.

Jupiter: The fifth planet in the solar system. Jupiter rules the astrological sign of Sagittarius. It rules Thursdays and is connected to the air and fire elements. Jupiter magick is good for abundance, prosperity, and success.

Mars: The fourth planet in the solar system. Mars rules the astrological signs of Aries and Leo. It rules Tuesday and is connected to fire. Mars magick is good for cursing, banishing, and boundary setting.

Mercury: The first planet in the solar system. Mercury rules the astrological signs of Gemini and Virgo. It rules Wednesday and is connected to air and water. Mercury magick is good for communication, business, and travel.

Moon: The moon isn't a planet, but a satellite of Earth. The moon rules the astrological sign of Cancer. It rules Monday and is connected to water. Moon magick is good for many things; it will vary depending on which phase the moon is in.

Neptune: The seventh planet in the solar system. Neptune rules the astrological sign of Pisces. It is connected to water. Neptune magick is good for clairvoyance, dreams, and creativity.

Pluto: This planet-that-is-not-a-planet is the last celestial body in our solar system. Pluto rules the astrological sign of Scorpio. It is connected to water. Pluto magick is good for Underworld rituals, transformation, and wealth.

Saturn: The sixth planet in the solar system. Saturn rules the astrological signs of Aquarius and Capricorn. It rules Saturday and is connected to earth and water. Saturn magick is good for ambition, boundaries, and strength.

Sun: The sun isn't a planet, but the center of our solar system. The sun rules the astrological sign of Leo. It rules Sunday and is connected with fire. Sun magick is good for many kinds of magick. The time of day, the month, and the time of the year are all possible ways the sun's magick can change.

Uranus: The eighth planet in the solar system. Uranus rules the astrological sign of Aquarius. It is connected to the element of air. Uranus magick is good for intuition, hope, and power.

Venus: The second planet in the solar system. Venus rules the astrological signs of Taurus and Libra. It rules Friday and is connected with earth. Venus magick is good for love, desire, and relationship.

ZODIAC

The zodiac and astrology have been used in combination with magick for thousands of years. In many cultures, when a child is born, their astrological chart is graphed and omens are given for the life they will lead. Just as the planets have an impact on our magick, so do the zodiacal signs.

The study of astrology is a huge area that takes a lifetime of study and dedication to learn. But you can utilize a basic understanding of the stars and their movements to help boost your rituals and spells.

The dates ruled by each zodiac sign vary year to year. When looking for your own sign, it is important to check the year you were born to make sure you've got the correct dates.

Aries (March 21–April 19): Ruled by the planet Mars and the spring equinox; ruler of Tuesday. Aries is a fire sign. The power of Aries is connected to ambition and action. It is the sign of independence, lust, and virility. It can also be fuel for jealousy, fear, and anger.

Taurus (April 20–May 20): Ruled by the planet Venus and the spring; ruler of Friday. Taurus is an earth sign. The power of Taurus is connected to comfort and grounding. It is the sign of pleasure, money, and security. It can also be fuel for laziness, stubbornness, and jealousy.

Gemini (May 21–June 21): Ruled by the planet Mercury and the early summer; ruler of Wednesday. Gemini is an air sign. The power of Gemini is connected to communication and intelligence. It is the sign of knowledge, learning, and community. It can also be fuel for distraction, mercurialness, and flip-flopping.

Cancer (June 22–July 22): Ruled by the moon and the summer solstice; ruler of Monday. Cancer is a water sign. The power of Cancer is connected to emotions, nurturing, and determination. It is the sign of romance, support, and protection. It can also be fuel for moodiness, secrets, and grudges.

Leo (July 23–August 22): Ruled by the sun and Lughnasadh; ruler of Sunday. Leo is a fire sign. The power of Leo is connected to ambition, power, and passion. It is the sign of leadership, determination, and affection. It can also be fuel for possessiveness, pride, and selfishness.

Virgo (August 23–September 22): Ruled by the planet Mercury and the late summer; ruler of Wednesday. Virgo is an earth sign. The power of Virgo is connected to abundance, success, and order. It is the sign of independence, analytics, and organization. It can also be fuel for nitpicking, shyness, and hyperfocus.

Libra (September 23–October 23): Ruled by the planet Venus and the fall equinox; ruler of Friday. Libra is an air sign. The power of Libra is connected to balance, attraction, and sensuality. It is the sign of beauty, cooperation, and fairness. It can also be fuel for selfishness, lack of boundaries, and lovesickness.

Scorpio (October 24–November 21): Ruled by the planet Pluto and Samhain; ruler of Tuesday. Scorpio is a water sign. The power of Scorpio is connected to sexuality, authority, and loyalty. It is the sign of passion, psychic abilities, and transformation. It can also be fuel for obsession, possessiveness, and distrust.

Sagittarius (November 22–December 21): Ruled by the planet Jupiter and the late autumn; ruler of Wednesday. Sagittarius is a fire sign. The power of Sagittarius is connected to freedom, optimism, and honesty. It is the sign of spirituality, travel, and growth. It can also be fuel for distractedness, danger, and a lack of boundaries.

Capricorn (December 22–January 19): Ruled by Saturn and the winter solstice; ruler of Thursday. Capricorn is an earth sign. The power of Capricorn is connected to ambition, discipline, and willpower. It is the sign of success, manifestation, and responsibility. It can also be fuel for status-climbing, negativity, and darkness.

Aquarius (January 20–February 18): Ruled by Uranus and the late winter; ruler of Saturday. Aquarius is an air sign. The power of Aquarius is connected to independence, determination, and intelligence. It is the sign of community, compassion, and wisdom. It can also be fuel for wishy-washiness, passive-aggression, and controlling behaviors.

 Pisces (February 19–March 20): Ruled by Neptune and Imbolc; ruler of Thursday. Pisces is a water sign. The power of Pisces is connected to intuition, compassion, and sensitivity. It is the sign of psychic ability, unity, and adaptability. It can also be fuel for sorrow, deceit, and lack of focus.

Planning with Correspondences

Using colors, angels, numbers, and more can also help your spells and rituals. My recommendation is to pay attention to correspondences when planning your rituals, especially spells, but try not to let them dictate every step of the process. Correspondences should make your rituals and spell workings easier, not keep you frozen waiting for the perfect timing or just-right ingredient.

There are so many ways to work with correspondences to improve your ceremonies and spells. It helps to pick one or two types of correspondences that you find interesting. Enjoy learning the ins and outs of all the different options.

COLORS

Our personal relationship to a color is an important and vital part of how we relate colors in our ceremonies and spells. There are innumerable amounts of colors in our world; it would be impossible to name them all. But there are nine colors most often mentioned in magickal texts. They are red, orange, yellow, green, blue, purple, and pink, along with black and white.

These colors have a lot of historical magickal context from cultures around the globe. Oftentimes, one culture's meaning of a color is the same or similar to another's. There are also a lot of modern color connotations that impact the way we relate to color. For example, gold is a color that many people around the world understand as a magickal symbol for wealth and money. This is because actual gold was the standard for money for many, many years. Gold has a value that can be tracked and traced and literally weighed. However, that is no longer the case in most modern countries. In the United States, we often use the color green for money spell work because the color of our paper money is green. The relationship between money and the color green is relatively new, but it is deeply ingrained in our culture.

It is good to understand some of the different cultural and historical color connections, but it is also important to understand your personal relationship to colors. Yellow is traditionally a color of happiness and success, but if you relate that color to a memory that is sad, it will be hard for you to use yellow in rituals that are intended to evoke joy.

Here are some common color correspondences.

- **Red:** This color is related to the south and the elements of fire and air. It is a color to use in rituals for anger, sex, passion, love, courage, focus, power, truth, assertiveness, determination, and ambition.
- **Orange:** This color is related to the south and the element of fire. It is a color to use in rituals for ambition, road opening, success, strength, power, taking action, confidence, creating order, positivity, and optimism.
- **Yellow:** This color is related to the east and the elements of air and fire. It is a color to use in rituals for joy, happiness, cooperation, community, creativity, imagination, the mind, stimulation, and willpower.
- **Green:** This color is related to the full moon, the north, the west, and the elements of earth and water. It is a color to use in rituals for abundance, prosperity, wealth, heart healing, generosity, business success, compassion, fertility, kindness, and grounding.
- **Blue:** This color is related to the west and the element of water. It is a color to use in rituals for intuition, clarity, communication, forgiveness, blessings, dream work, emotional awareness, clearing, forgiveness, and purification.

- **Purple:** This color is related to the west and the element of water. It is a color to use in rituals for power, success, prophecy, psychic abilities, truth, transformation, astral travel, wealth, and increasing personal skills.
- **Pink:** This color is related to the elements of air and fire. It is a color to use in rituals for romantic love, happiness, harmony, compassion, affection, romance, clearing stress, marriage and commitment, attraction, and sensuality.
- **Black:** This color is related to the new moon, the north, and the element of earth. It is a color to use in rituals for protection, keeping things hidden, psychic abilities, dark or new moon rituals, banishment, and Underworld and death work.
- **White:** This color is related to all the directions and all the elements. It is often said that this color can be used as a replacement for any other color in a magickal pinch. It is a color of blessings, balance, wisdom, and clarity.

STONES

Gems, stones, and crystals have really grown in popularity over the last few years, and it's no real surprise because they are beautiful! The good news is you don't have to invest in expensive and rare gems for them to really impact your magick.

Stones and crystals that are in alignment with your ritual or magickal goal can add power to the working, but a stone that you found at the beach or a crystal that was gifted to you are just as powerful.

When possible, learn where your stones, gems, and crystals came from. In some places dangerous practices are used for mining, and miners can be exposed to life-threatening chemicals and environments. Some mines even use child labor. So, ask questions!

There are thousands of types of stones that you can use in your rituals, but there are some stones that are more commonly found and can be used in a lot of different types of magickal rites. I've included some of the most common stones in the following chart.

I've kept stones that have many variations off this list. There are too many variations of these stones, and each one is different and unique.

Stone	Element(s)	Planet(s)	Zodiac Sign(s)	Day(s) of the Week	Direction(s)	Main Energy
Amethyst	Water	Neptune	Aquarius, Capricorn	Saturday, Thursday	Northeast	Clairvoyance
Aquamarine	Water	Moon, Neptune	Aquarius, Aries			Inspiration
Bloodstone	Fire	Mars	Aries, Scorpio	Tuesday	East	Prosperity
Blue lace agate	Air, water	Mercury	Pisces		Northeast	Clarity
Carnelian	Fire	Mercury, sun	Aries, Leo	Sunday, Thursday	South	Prosperity
Citrine	Fire	Mars, Mercury	Aries, Leo		East	Abundance
Desert rose	Air	Venus	Libra		Southwest	Beauty
Diamond	Fire	Mars, Venus	Libra, Taurus	Saturday, Sunday	East	Fidelity
Emerald	Earth	Jupiter, Venus	Cancer, Taurus	Monday, Friday	North	Love
Fluorite	Earth, water	Mercury, Neptune	Capricorn, Pisces		North, South	Clairvoyance
Garnet	Fire	Mars, Pluto	Aries, Leo	Tuesday	South, Southwest	Sexuality

Stone	Element(s)	Planet(s)	Zodiac Sign(s)	Day(s) of the Week	Direction(s)	Main Energy
Hematite	Earth, fire	Mars, Saturn	Aries, Capricorn	Saturday		Protection
Jade	Earth, water	Neptune, Venus	Aquarius, Libra		Northeast	Abundance
Jet	Earth, water	Pluto, Saturn	Capricorn	Saturday	East	Prosperity
Labradorite	Water	Neptune, Pluto	Leo, Sagittarius	Saturday	Northeast	Clairvoyance
Lodestone	Water	Venus	Gemini	Wednesday	North	Prosperity
Malachite	Earth	Venus	Capricorn, Taurus		North	Abundance
Obsidian	Fire	Pluto, Saturn	Capricorn, Scorpio		North, South	Protection
Onyx	Fire	Mars, Mercury	Aquarius, Leo		Northeast	Grounding
Opal	Air, water	Mercury, moon	Cancer, Scorpio	Wednesday	South	Inspiration
Peridot	Earth, fire	Mercury, sun	Leo, Scorpio		North	Abundance
Pyrite	Fire	Mars	Taurus			Prosperity

Stone	Element(s)	Planet(s)	Zodiac Sign(s)	Day(s) of the Week	Direction(s)	Main Energy
Rose quartz	Water	Venus	Libra, Taurus	Friday	Southwest	Love
Ruby	Fire	Mars, sun	Aries, Leo	Friday	Southwest	Love
Sapphire	Water	Moon, Neptune	Cancer, Pisces	Monday, Thursday	Northeast	Luck
Selenite	Water	Moon	Cancer, Taurus		North	Harmony
Smoky quartz	Earth, fire		Capricorn, Libra		Southwest	Protection
Sodalite	Air, water	Mercury, Venus	Sagittarius		South	Attraction
Tiger's eye	Fire	Sun	Gemini, Leo	Sunday		Prosperity
Topaz	Fire	Mercury, sun	Leo, Scorpio	Sunday, Tuesday	Southeast	Communication
Tourmaline	Earth, water	Saturn, sun	Capricorn, Libra			Protection
Turquoise	Earth, water	Jupiter, moon	Aquarius, Scorpio	Saturday, Wednesday	Southwest	Luck

NUMBERS

If you think about it, math is a form of magick. It is an ancient system that allows us to discover truth and learn more about the world around us. The system of numbers we use now, with ten symbols making up all of the combinations, started in India in the sixth or seventh century.[8]

Numerology is the study of numbers and how those numbers impact the world around us. Pythagoras was a Greek philosopher who originally posited that there was a connection between the greater world and numbers, originally by connecting numbers to musical notes. He would use the numbers in people's birthdates as a way of discerning what their personalities might be.[9]

Modern numerology is a descendant of this concept made popular by Pythagoras.

1. Connected to Sunday, the colors gold and white, and the element of fire. Magickally this number connects to the individual, ambition, and the beginnings of things. This is the number of self-work, willpower, and leadership.

2. Connected to Monday, the colors green and white, and the element of water. Magickally this number connects to partnership, balance, and the duality of things. This is the number of patience, romance, emotional support, and love.

3. Connected to Wednesday, the colors green and purple, and the element of fire. Magickally this number connects to triplicity and cycles. This is the number of luck, psychic abilities, balance, connections, and communication.

4. Connected to the colors blue and brown and the element of earth. Magickally this number connects to stability, business, patience, and boundaries. This is the number of building and solid foundations, clearing obstacles, and manifestation.

---

8   The Editors of Encyclopaedia Britannica, "Hindu-Arabic numerals," *Encyclopaedia Britannica*, last modified September 8, 2017, https://www.britannica.com/topic/Hindu-Arabic-numerals.

9   O'Connor and Robertson, "Pythagoras of Samos."

5. Connected to Tuesday, the colors red and white, and the element of air. Magickally this number connects to action, energy, and change. This is the number of conflicts, fear, and the senses.

6. Connected to Friday, the colors blue and pink, and the element of earth. Magickally this number connects to balance, comfort, harmony, and the home. This is the number of luck, love, relationships, and money.

7. Connected to Saturday, the colors green and purple, and the element of water. Magickally this number connects to initiation, accomplishments, spirituality, and success. This is the number of truth, healing, awareness, and spiritual growth.

8. Connected to Thursday, the colors black and orange, and the element of earth. Magickally this number connects to abundance, power, and stability. This is the number of pride, discipline, authority, ambition, and spiritual pursuits.

9. Connected to Friday and Monday, the colors pink and red, and the element of fire. Magickally this number connects to protection, psychic skills, healing, and courage. This is the number of the mind, wisdom, beginnings, and endings.

10. This is both number one and number zero. It is a symbol of beginnings and ends, of everything and nothing. It is connected to blue and black and the element of spirit. Magickally this number connects to cycles, death, and rebirth. This is the number of fertility and completion.

ANGELS

Many Witches work with or call upon angels in their spells, rituals, and rites. Angels are much older than Christianity, although in our dominant culture many assume angels to be of Christian origin. From a Witchcraft perspective, the archangels are the entities that are most often asked for help in rites.

I really debated including angels here. I personally don't work with angels in my Witchcraft, but I've noticed an increasing interest in them. I think it is important to have information about any entity you might encounter in your Witchcraft, so I have included some information here about the most commonly called upon archangels.

- ◆ **Gabriel:** Connected to the earth and the moon; the astrological signs of Aquarius, Cancer, Pisces, and Scorpio; as well as Monday and dusk. Gabriel's colors are blue, green, and white. Call upon this archangel when you need help with dreams, healing, renewal, and truth.
- ◆ **Michael:** Connected to the planet Mercury and the sun; the astrological signs of Aries, Leo, and Sagittarius; as well as noon and the south. Michael's colors are copper, red, and white. Call upon this archangel when you need help with protection, strength, willpower, and justice.
- ◆ **Raphael:** Connected to the planet Mercury and the sun; the astrological signs of Aquarius, Gemini, and Libra; as well as Wednesday and the dawn. Raphael's colors are blue, gold, white, and yellow. Call upon this archangel when you need help with harmony, healing, support, and safe travel.
- ◆ **Uriel:** Connected to the planet Venus; the astrological signs of Capricorn, Taurus, and Virgo; as well as Friday and midnight. Uriel's colors are brown, gold, green, and white. Call upon this archangel when you need help with divination and clairvoyance, learning and teaching, as well as wisdom and wealth.

SECTION TWO
Bone

Bone is what gives our body form. It is the underlying structure that makes it so we can walk and move and turn our heads. Our bones are the outline of our body. Bones are strong and sturdy; they are a thing we can depend on. Bones can break, but they repair themselves.

The Bones of Ritual are the earth-like influences on the ritual. It is the form, the function, and the actual steps the ritual must follow. Without the Bones of Ritual there would be no ritual.

If the Breath of Ritual is the most important step, the Bones of Ritual are the real-world pieces that are needed to make the ritual happen. The Bones of Ritual show us the actual steps we need to take, what we need to do, and in what order we need to do them.

In this section, we will go over all of the steps of setting up your ceremony. I will go into detail about creating sacred space, what tools are necessary, and what options you have when performing rituals.

The Bones of Ritual are the physical steps, actions, plots, and outlines. The Bones of Ritual are the actual parts of the ritual flow, the magick that will be performed. This is the part of the planning process that gives shape to the thing you are creating. It is in this part of the planning process that we will need to remember the work we did with the Breath of Ritual. We might find ourselves returning to that part of the planning over and over again in order to help the Bones of Ritual find their best structure and form. This is the part in the planning when the idea of a ritual becomes an actual plan.

The Bones of Ritual are what makes ritual possible.

Tools: Do You Need Them?

In many magickal traditions, the use of tools is commonplace. But having tools isn't necessary for a solid magickal practice or to create sacred space. Even though tools aren't required to practice Witchcraft, there is something to be said about having ritual tools—ones that are only used for magickal purposes.

When we have dedicated and consecrated ceremonial tools, it helps us step into the right mindset and energy when creating our rites. A consecrated ritual cup will feel different than a regular coffee cup. It's like the Holy Grail versus a regular wine glass.

Some Witchcraft practitioners believe that you need to make or craft as many of your tools as possible. There is something to be said for this. When you craft tools with your own hands, it gives you a link to that tool. It becomes a personal extension of you, even without ritual consecration. That tool is a part of you.

However, some tools are really difficult to make on your own. For example, without a forge you're unlikely to be able to make an athame. And even with a forge, if you don't know what you're doing, it's likely to be a lot more trouble than it's worth. Purchasing a tool from a maker, shop, or even a thrift store is perfectly fine. What's more important than crafting your own tool is finding a tool that you love and want to work with or see on your altar for magickal purposes.

There are some tools that are traditional to modern Witchcraft. But with that being said, ultimately, your body is the only real tool that you need. And you don't have to use a consecrated tool in your rituals; anything you have will work in a pinch. As we go through the potential ritual tools, I will share bodily alternatives or stand-in tools that you can use as a replacement in any rite.

ALTARS

There is a lot of confusion that comes up around altars. At my witchy shop one of the most frequently asked questions is how to set up an altar the "right way." The truth is, there isn't just one way to set up an altar. It depends on what the altar is for and if it is connected to any specific tradition.

General Purpose Altars

A general purpose altar is a permanent place where you spend spiritual time and perform ongoing work on a regular basis. This might be a place where you meditate, light candles, burn incense, or are in communion with the world around you. A general purpose altar could also be a place where you have small shrines, divination tools, or ongoing spell work. These altars could be small, like the edge of a bookshelf or the corner of a desk. These types of altars could also take up the space of an entire room. A general purpose altar is set up all the time and is used for a variety of reasons.

Working Altars

Typically, working altars are temporary. They are the places where you step in, do what needs to be done, and then put it all away. Working altars might be the specific location for a spell working, or they could be set up for one ritual. A working altar is a temporary set up and is used for a specific purpose.

Seasonal Altars

A seasonal altar is where you celebrate the turning of the Wheel and seasonal celebrations. You might follow the traditional Wheel of the Year or create your own. A seasonal altar should hold decorations, colors, and trinkets that match what is going on in the world around you. It is a place where you can connect with the current energy. A seasonal altar could be the same place as a general purpose altar. It could also be a working altar put up for a specific amount of time and then taken down and cleaned up. A seasonal altar can either be temporary or permanent and is used to honor the turning of the Wheel.

Altars of Veneration

Altars of veneration, also called shrines, are the places you set up for your worship or devotional practices. These altars might be for ancestors, deities, or other spiritual beings. Ideally, an altar of veneration will contain items that would appeal to the entity the altar is dedicated to; you would want to use colors, offerings, incense, and decorations that would appeal to that entity. An altar of veneration is up permanently and is used for a specific purpose.

—◆◆—

As you may have noticed, because I keep repeating it over and over again, different Witchcraft traditions have differing rules about how to do things. An altar is one of the big ones. Lineage Witchcraft Traditions will have rules for altars like:

- Which direction the altar should be placed or facing.
- Where the altar tools should be placed on the altar.
- Where deity statues or images should be placed.
- What deity statues or images are used.
- If an altar cloth is used and what color(s) it might be.
- If flowers should be used and where they are placed.
- Where High Priest (HP), High Priestess (HPS), and participants should stand around the altars.
- Which tools are included for which rituals.

If your altar isn't connected to a specific tradition or lineage, it can literally be set up any way you desire. What's more important than what goes where is that the altar appeals to *you*.

Any altar that you create should be kept clean. Don't let your altar spaces get cluttered, dusty, or filled with a bunch of used incense and old spell remnants. If need be, clear off your altars, cleanse them, and burn any old or unwanted items at least once a year. I recommend the summer solstice.

When setting up working altars for rituals and ceremonies, make sure there is enough space to get around the altar. The surface of the altar needs to be big enough to fit all the items you will be using. You will need to decide what tools go on the altar and if they need to be consecrated. You'll also need to decide if this altar space will be up all the time or if you will take it down and store the pieces between ritual workings.

ATHAME

The athame is a double-edged ritual knife. The word *athame* didn't appear in any writings until 1949, in the book *High Magic's Aid* by Gerald Gardner.[10] In the book *The Witch's Athame*, author Jason Mankey explores the history of the word *athame* and suggests that the first use of a similar word comes from The Key of Solomon; through a series of mistranslations, we ended up with the word *athame* as our magickal blade.[11]

The pronunciation of the word *athame* isn't agreed upon. In some parts of the world, it is pronounced as ATH-a-may, while in others it is said as a-THOM-ay, and I've even heard it as AH-tame and ath-am-EE. There's a theory that the different pronunciations come from different regions and English dialects, but I think it's just as likely that many practitioners from the '80s and '90s first came across the word in a book and then decided for ourselves how to say it out loud.

In some traditions the athame has a black handle and is a representation of masculine energy. This tool is used as a symbol for the element of air in some circles, while in others it is a symbol for the element of fire. I could argue that both of these elemental alignments make sense, so it will be up to you and your practice (or tradition) to determine which element feels like it is in alignment with the athame.

In the book *The Elements of Ritual*, author Deborah Lipp explains that when A. E. Waite was creating the tarot deck that has become known as the Rider-Waite-Smith deck, he connected the Swords to air and the Wands to fire as a deliberate attempt to obfuscate the truth of his oathbound traditional learning, which had the elemental correspondences reversed and the knife being the tool of fire.[12] This has become a bit of folklore on its own, but it's uncertain if this is the truth. In the book *The Golden Dawn* by Israel Regardie, the Ace of Swords is called the "Root of the Powers of Air," and

---

10   Mankey, *The Witch's Athame*, 2.

11   Mankey, *The Witch's Athame*, 20–22.

12   Lipp, *The Elements of Ritual*, 7.

the Ace of Wands is called the "Root of the Powers of Fire." So again, the arguments for the tools and the directions could go either way.[13]

The argument for the athame being connected to air makes sense because we use the athame to cut through the air or etheric threads. The athame is a tool of discernment and clarity. These are all attributes of the element of air. However, it could also be connected to the element of fire because a blade is forged in fire—it is literally born from fire. The athame sends energy to cast a circle, which is often described as a circle of fire. It is a tool of will and power and these are attributes of the element of fire.

I don't think there is one true answer here. I think both are true and neither are true. It's more about your personal relationship with the tools and the elements, as well as the rules of the tradition you might practice in.

As mentioned, in magickal space, the athame is used to delineate space, direct energy, send energy, focus power, and cut through energy. It can also be used as a tool to carve candles and other ritual supplies.

When you consecrate an athame for your personal magickal use, you might carve or engrave words, symbols, runes, Theban script, or sigils into the handle or blade of the knife.

Athame Alternatives
The first two fingers of your dominant hand can be used to direct and send energy.

BELL
A bell is used mainly in traditional Wiccan rituals. It can be used to clear energy, shake up stagnant energy, call energy, or banish energy. In some lineages of Traditional Witchcraft, the size and shape of the bell does matter, but for the most part there aren't specific rules on the size, shape, or type of bell you use. I've even seen singing bowls or chimes used in more eclectic practices.

---

13   Regardie, *The Golden Dawn*, 683.

Bell Alternatives

An alarm or ringtone from your phone can be used in place of a bell.

BOLINE

The origins of the boline are supposedly Celtic or Druidic in origin. There is some lore that the Druids would cut sacred herbs with a sickle-shaped blade. The boline is a sacred tool to be used outside of ritual space in order to collect items for ritual. The first mention of the boline is in occultist A. E. Waite's *The Book of Ceremonial Magic*, where he refers to the boline as the "most important" tool.[14]

The use of the boline in modern Witchcraft is still connected to the harvesting of herbs and sacred plants for use in ritual and magick. It is an excellent tool to use when wildcrafting.

BOOK OF SHADOWS

A Book of Shadows (or BoS) is a cross between a personal diary and a scientific journal. In my opinion, your BoS is the most important Witchcraft physical tool. A BoS is the place where you keep track of your spells, rituals, and magickal workings. This is where you track all ritual components, from timing to ingredients to the exact words used. A BoS can also serve as a personal journal where you write down your experiences and feelings and keep track of what is generally going on in your life.

Your personal feelings and life experiences will impact your magick and rituals. By tracking both of these pieces of your world, you will get a better idea of the trends in your Witchcraft and what your expectations should be for future magickal work.

The term *Book of Shadows* is a relatively new word, only coming into use in the 1950s.[15] However, writing down magickal concepts, spells, and ideas is an ancient practice. The word *grimoire* is another term for a BoS, although much older; it's a French word that refers to books of magick. Many Witches prefer the term *grimoire* over Book of Shadows.

---

14   Mankey, *The Witch's Athame*, 133–39.
15   Mankey, *The Witch's Book of Shadows*, 7.

I think every Witch needs their own personal BoS as a way of tracking their magick. However, it's not uncommon for covens to also keep a group BoS. In a coven's BoS, you will find the coven rules, notes or minutes from coven meetings, details of rituals and spells, as well as which members were in attendance at what gatherings.

As you can imagine, a coven's BoS provides a lot of detailed magickal information about a group of Witches. It is not something that you would want to fall into the wrong hands, but that is really true of any BoS. Most covens will use coveners' magickal names rather than their mundane names to keep things as anonymous as possible.

Some Witches will write their entire BoS in code or alternative languages. The Theban script is one of those coded writings. Although there isn't a spoken language for Theban, it is a well-known written language in magickal circles. Only those "in the know" would be able to decipher Theban script.

Theban script was created in Germany during the 1700s. It was likely created as a cipher or coded writing for grimoires. When it was included in Agrippa's book *Third Book of Occult Philosophy*, it became more popular and has been connected to several occult and magickal systems ever since.[16]

My favorite Book of Shadows in pop culture is the book they use in the 1998 movie *Practical Magic*. It is a large, leather-bound book filled with decades of writing, herb clippings, dried plants, bits of bugs and animals, and so much more. It's not just a BoS, but a work of art. This is the book I aspire to have, but my personal book is much simpler.

The BoS that I have used since 1995 is a plain black three-ring binder. It has some images clipped out and glued to the front and the back. There are writings and rituals that I have tracked and used since the mid-1990s. When it felt necessary, I've pulled pages out of this book and burned them. And I've added more lined paper (a lot more) over the years. It ain't pretty, but it does the trick.

In some lineages of Witchcraft and Wicca, you don't get access to your tradition's BoS until you reach a certain level of initiation or elevation. And

---

16   Mankey, *The Witch's Book of Shadows*, 169.

even then, it isn't handed over to you—you are required to write it all down in your own hand, which is a serious amount of writing in most traditions.

Of course, back in the day it made sense that your BoS needed to be handwritten; there weren't any other options. But now there are lots of Witches that use the notes app in their phones, Google Docs, or Word to write and track their magick and spells. Although there is a bit less romanticism in an electronic BoS, there is an ease and simplicity in being able to track everything electronically. Just make sure you keep a backup.

Just like a personal diary or journal, a BoS isn't a book you would just share with anyone. In most cases, I would say don't share it with *anyone*. In fact, many Witchcraft traditions have a curse written on the first page of the BoS that anyone reading the book that was not specifically invited to will walk in the shadows forever.

Consider yourselves warned.

Book of Shadows Alternative

A Book of Shadows doesn't have to be a fancy leather-bound journal. You could use Google Docs or Word to write your ritual notes. You could use the notes app on your smartphone. Any place you can write and store your experiences can become your Book of Shadows.

BESOM

A besom is a fancy magickal word for a ritual, or Witch's, broom. There's nothing as classic as the image of a Witch and her broom, right? Brooms and besoms are mainly used to clear, cleanse, and banish energy. However, they can also serve as guardians of liminal spaces, like front doors: besoms can create liminal boundaries, represent thresholds, or even be used for cursing spells.

Traditionally, the Witch's broom would have been made with a sturdy wooden handle and either thin twig bristles or straw-type bristles. Depending on what you want to use your broom for, you can pick woods or plant materials that help your broom have the right kind of energy.

There is a lot of folklore and superstition around brooms and household magick, most of which have to do with giving or taking luck. Here are just a few:

- Don't take your broom with you when you move from one house to another, and never use a broom that has been left behind in a dwelling you are moving into.
- When a broom falls, it means unexpected company is coming.
- Store your broom with the bristles up for good luck.
- Never lend your broom to another person or they will steal your good luck.
- Sweeping over another person's feet (intentionally or accidentally) will bring them bad luck, or even death.

Besom Alternative

A regular kitchen broom will work in place of a special consecrated broom. Heck, a Swiffer can work in a pinch!

CAULDRON

The cauldron is the Witchcraft tool for the element of spirit or aether. It is connected to the location of Center. The cauldron, more than any other magickal tool, shows up in history, folklore, and myth, and not always in relationship to Witches. It is always a tool of change, unending blessings, and renewal. The cauldron is a tool of transformation: what goes into the cauldron comes out changed.

In ritual the cauldron can hold your potions and all of your potion's ingredients. It can also hold ritual fires, be used to burn incense, and be a receptacle for papers you want to burn.

In most modern circles, the cauldron is made of cast iron. Cast iron is easy to use, will heat safely, and can be used for a wide variety of purposes. But cauldrons are also made from brass, ceramic, copper, bronze, and even silver. If you are in the market for a cauldron, make sure you know what metals it is made from. Some metals are toxic or have a low melting point. If you make any assumptions about the metal, it could cause you trouble or injury.

Cauldron Alternative

A nice big kitchen pot makes a perfect cauldron. Just make sure if you do anything in your cauldron that could make you ill, you don't use that pot for cooking ever again.

CHALICE

The chalice is a magickal cup, much like the Holy Grail, only with less wars fought over it. The sacred cup is a symbol that repeats in cultures and religions all over the world. In modern Witchcraft the chalice serves as a representation for the element of water on altars and during ritual. This tool is used during ceremonies for drinking and offering libations. It is also a tool for turning a mundane drink into a magickal one.

In some traditions the chalice represents the feminine and the athame is the masculine. Personally, I am not a huge fan of this symbology. For one thing, it supports a gender binary, which is boring and not representative of the full spectrum. But also, it reinforces the idea that the feminine is receptive and will receive the masculine within it. And it boils masculine energy down to a projecting and aggressive energy; having a blade representing masculinity might have worked in the 1950s, but it doesn't anymore.

The chalice is an important symbol in Christian mythology too. In certain Christian traditions the size, shape, and measurements of the ceremonial chalice must meet specific specifications. Modern Witchcraft and Wiccan systems don't seem to have the same rules around these things, but it is an interesting addition to a ritual altar; having a chalice meet specific dimensions plays into the use of sacred geometry in magick.

A chalice is simply a cup that has been consecrated to become a sacred tool. In formal ritual, using a goblet-style cup makes sense, but you can also consecrate a coffee mug or water glass. By doing this you can turn your simple daily rituals, like morning coffee or drinking water with your medications and vitamins, into more sacred routines.

Chalice Alternative

Any glass or cup from your kitchen can serve as a chalice. Even a paper cup can work in a pinch.

CORDS

Many witches use cords in their practices. In some traditions cords are used as a marker of your status in the coven or group. Different color cords suggest different roles or levels of elevation in coven status. These cords are worn around the waist during rituals.

It's not uncommon for a coven or group to take a "Witch's measure" when initiation happens. Cords are used to literally measure the physical body. This is done as a form of sympathetic magick. This is one of those romantic practices from back in the old days. The story goes that a coven would take a new member's measure and the leader of the group would hold the physical cords in their possession. If that Witch turned against her coven, the leader could then curse her using the cords of her measure.

I've had my measure taken three different times in my life as a Witch—so far, at least. And I'll tell you what, it is a rather scary experience. It is a bit like handing over a piece of yourself to someone else. This is why it is so important to have full trust in anyone offering you initiation. Giving away your measure is not to be taken lightly.

Witches also love cord and knot magick. There are lots of spells that require cords of different colors and lengths and ties being made in a specific order to cast spells.

INCENSE BURNER

A censer, incense burner, ash catcher, or fireproof container will work perfectly as a receptacle to burn incense in. It's common to see a censer-type incense burner in traditions like Wicca, but really anything that is firesafe will do the job—although an incense burner without any incense to burn really won't do much for your rituals.

Because scent is such a powerful trigger for our spiritual and emotional bodies, incense is often used in rituals. Specific formulas are handed down from coven to coven as part of their magickal lineage. The scent of certain ritual incense can put you in a ceremonial mood. A scented smoke in the air also changes the look and feel of a space. A room glowing with candles and a soft cloud of incense looks rather magickal and mysterious, and this feeds our magickal selves.

However, increasingly, people have a negative response to incense and scent. At public gatherings or events, there is often a request for things to be scent-free. When working in a small coven or solitary situation, you can do whatever you like.

There are lots of forms of incense that can be used in ritual. They all work perfectly well, but some types of incense burn better than others.

- **Cone:** Made from powder or loose incense shavings that are pressed into the form of a cone. This shape burns easily and can be purchased in a variety of scents. It will put out a small amount of smoke. A small brass cone incense holder works best for this type of incense.
- **Dhoop:** Made from powder or loose incense shavings that are pressed into the form of a stick. This stick-style incense will be thin, thick, or spiral shaped. Although difficult to light, this form of incense tends to be more heavily scented and puts more smoke into the air. An ash catcher or cauldron filled with sand works best for this type of incense.
- **Herbs:** Dried herbs can be burned as incense. They can be placed directly on an incense charcoal and burned with ease, just make sure the herbs are nontoxic and you aren't allergic to them. Herb incense will smoke differently depending on the plant. The scent of the smoke will also vary and may not match what the plant smells like when dried or fresh. This form of incense tends to put out a lot of smoke.
- **Loose:** Made from herbs, resins, or incense shavings. This type of incense may be very fine, like powder, or come with big chunks of resins or herbs. It's typically made with a blend of scents. This style

of incense won't really burn on its own, unless it is a fine self-igniting powder that is tightly packed, but it will burn easily on top of an incense charcoal. The amount of smoke will vary greatly depending on the ingredients in the mixture. The ingredients will also impact the scent.

+ **Resin:** Most forms of incense are actually just the resin of a plant. Many plants and trees secrete a syrup-like substance that, when dried, makes a lovely incense. This form of incense will need to be burned on an incense charcoal. This style of incense tends to put out a lot of smoke and a strong scent.

+ **Stick:** Similar to dhoop incense, but stick incense has an actual stick within its core. The compressed self-igniting incense powder is formed over the stick and will need to be burned in an ash catcher. This shape burns easily and can be purchased in a variety of scents. They are the most common form of incense; I've even seen them for sale at gas stations. Stick incense will put out a small amount of smoke.

MIRROR

The mirror is one of my favorite magickal tools in ritual, and I believe it is the most underutilized. Mirrors across cultures are known as tools that hold, collect, and project energy or visions. There are lots of superstitions connected to the dead and mirrors too; mirrors are like portals, and it serves you to be cautious and careful around them.

In modern Witchcraft the mirror isn't associated with any specific direction or element. It might even be considered a secondary tool, but it is an extremely powerful one. It is traditional to cover magickal mirrors in black cloth when they are not in use.

During the Victorian era, the psychomanteum was a dark chamber that had a mirror inside.[17] It was used to communicate with spirits of the dead. A silver mirror or black mirror could be used in a psychomanteum.

---

17   Mueller, *The Witch's Mirror*, 139.

There are typically two types of mirrors used in Witchcraft:

+ **Silver Mirror:** Antique mirrors had silver in their reflecting coating, but that isn't true anymore. However, the term *silver mirror* remains. A silver mirror is connected to the full moon and Goddess energy. It is most often used for positive magick, calling in the good and repelling the bad.
+ **Black Mirror:** Black mirrors are coated with a black paint rather than silver. They are not used for seeing reflections, but for seeing beyond them. Black mirrors are traditionally used for scrying or seeing, but they could also be used for deep spiritual work, past-life exploration, and working with spirits.

Another form of mirror magick is in the use of mirror boxes. These items are used in spellwork to perform reversing magick, to stop or bind someone from doing harm to other people. With a mirror box you would place an image or a poppet of the person you are doing the spellwork on inside the box. Any energy or magick they put into the world will be "reflected" back to them.

The outer shape of the mirror can also influence the magickal uses, as can whether the mirror is convex or concave. Mirrors can be charged for specific uses and purposes, but even regular mirrors that aren't specifically used for ceremonies hold magickal potential.

Mirror Alternative

Any mirror can work for mirror rituals, from a small hand mirror to a regular bathroom mirror. Just be sure to cleanse any regular household mirrors after rituals to clear the energy.

PENTACLE

The pentacle, although one of the most recognized tools, is the most misunderstood tool of modern Witchcraft. In fact, I know a lot of Witches that don't use a pentacle on their altars or in their magickal work at all. In modern Witchcraft the pentacle is used as a representation of the element of earth.

The pentacles that reside on our altars are typically made of metal or clay. They charge objects with power and help ground ritual participants.

The pentacle is more than a symbol of earth that sits on an altar. So much more. The pentacle is a connection to your physical body. A pentacle is a five-pointed star, and so are we.[18] Our legs, arms, and head make us a sacred symbol of earth. The pentacle is what keeps us connected to this power. In ritual, when the pentacle sits in the middle of the altar, all ritual participants can place their hands on the pentacle as a way to connect, ground, and restore their energy.

It's not uncommon to see Witches wearing jewelry with an engraved pentacle, or to see it on banners or tapestries as decoration. The symbols of the pentacle and pentagram have become the modern symbol of the Witch. It's a way to hide who we are in plain sight. I've seen a lot of folks working regular jobs with this symbol of their faith hanging from a chain on their neck.

Pentacle Alternative

If you have no other option, draw a pentacle on a piece of paper and use it as a stand-in on your altar.

STAFF

Some say as the sword is to the athame, the staff is to the wand. However, others say as the sword is to the athame, the staff is to the stang. This tool can be used to send and direct energy. And it can also be used as a central component to ritual, becoming the crossroads in ceremony. It is a tool that unites the different realms. Depending on how you use it, the staff can serve as a combination of wand and stang.

STANG

This tool is a staff with a V-shaped split at the top, almost looking like horns. The stang is an important tool in some Traditional Witchcraft sys-

---

18   To be specific, the pentacle is a five-pointed star with a circle around it, while the pentagram is just the star.

tems, especially those based off the teachings of Robert Cochrane, who was a popular English occultist in the 1960s. Cochrane referred to the stang as the supreme implement. This tool is used to direct energy, serves as the crossroads in ritual, aids in realm travels, and serves as a symbol of the Horned God during ritual.[19]

Staff/Stang Alternatives

Your full body can be used as a stang, as can a kitchen broom. However, when a stang is called for, you need the focus of that magickal tool and it is highly suggested that you seek one out. If you can perform the ceremony outdoors, a tree can also serve as a stang.

SWORD

The ritual sword is much like the athame. They are used for the same purposes, except the sword is much larger and more cumbersome in ritual. It's pretty typical to use the sword for casting a circle, but it is rarely used for other pieces of ritual when you would use an athame. I have been told that the athame is the tool of the Witch, while the sword is the tool of the coven.

Based on writings from the Golden Dawn, the sword is called for when the ritualist needs more power or strength, as well as for banishing evil.[20] It's almost as if size does matter when it comes to a blade and directing magickal energy.

There aren't any specific rules when it comes to the type or style of sword used for ritual purposes. But I do have a rule based on my personal experience. I have a ritual sword that was gifted to me. It is a big, heavy sword with intricate designs carved into the pommel. I absolutely love it. However, it is really heavy. Like, so heavy that I can't lift it using only one arm. It is not an ideal tool for ritual because it is so cumbersome; it does not work for casting a circle because my focus is on holding up the tool and not on directing my power.

---

19   Mankey, *The Witch's Altar*, 44.
20   Regardie, *The Golden Dawn*, 47.

So, if you want a sword, choose one that you love the look of, but also make sure that it is something you can use with ease.

WAND

A magician and their wand—it's a pretty classic image. Magick and wands always seem to go together. In modern Witchcraft, wands are used to delineate space and direct energy. They serve as an extension of the Witch, allowing their power to flow farther and stronger than the practitioner might be able to do on their own.

A wand can be metal, stone, or clay, but the most common and traditional form of a wand is made from wood. Occasionally the wood contains a metal core that serves as conductor of the energy. The types of wood used for a wand will change the correspondence of energy that wand carries. Different types of wood are good for different types of magick.

Traditionally the wand serves as the representation of the element of fire. But much like the athame, this correspondence can be debated. The connection between fire and wands is seen in the tarot as created by A. E. Waite. However, in other systems, the wand is connected to the element of air. And, just like with the athame, we could make a solid argument for both sides.

The relationship with the element of fire comes from the Golden Dawn; the wand directs energy, which is fire in the form of energy, and they often contain a core of metal for directing that energy. The relationship with the element of air is a little less solid; one could argue that the branches of the tree are in the sky, the wind blows through them, and the air curls around them, which gives wands a connection to the air in a very real way.

Wand Alternative

The first two fingers of your dominant hand can be used in place of a wand.

CONSECRATION

To consecrate something is to make it holy or sacred. With the tools of Witchcraft, this is done through a magickal rite. In order to consecrate something, we first have to ritually cleanse it to make it ready. Then we ritually charge it with its new magickal purpose. In some traditions, a consecrated tool should never be touched by anyone other than the practitioner who consecrated it. In other traditions, it is allowable for coven members to touch your consecrated tools. And there are also traditions where none of it matters, and hey, even consecrating your tools isn't necessary! Your mileage may vary.

When there is a well-known "rule" in Witchcraft, there is always someone happy to break that rule, ignore that rule, or tell you why that rule is wrong. This is where your discernment and personal practice really comes into play. Remember the Three Keys of Witchcraft?

You might choose to consecrate a tool for only ritual use, or you might consecrate a tool to use for everyday purposes to bring more magick into a seemingly mundane part of your life. Through the ritual of consecration, you can turn a mundane object into a magickal tool.

Cleansing and Consecrating a Ritual Tool

Now that you've learned all about ritual and magickal tools, it is time to cleanse and consecrate one for your own ritual use! The good news is you can pick anything from the list of magickal tools for this process. If you're feeling like you want some extra credit, you can pick multiple tools! If you'd like to cleanse and consecrate multiple tools, you can do them all at the same time or perform the ritual multiple times.

When performing this ritual, you might want to call on specific deities. Determine this beforehand and make sure you have a representation of that Godd on your altar space.

Supplies

The new ritual tool to consecrate, a bowl of salt, two bowls of water, a bowl of soil, incense in a burner, a candle in a candleholder, and a lighter or matches.

Setup

Create an altar with all of the supplies displayed to your liking. You may want to add other decorations to the altar; allow your intuition to help you determine how to set up your space. Be sure to have the new ritual tool in the center.

Ritual

Perform a cleansing and grounding. Choose one from this book or come up with your own.

When you feel ready, step into the middle of your ritual space, facing your altar. Using the first two fingers of your dominant hand, draw up energy from the earth and begin directing that energy around you in a circle. Finish by drawing that energy up above you and below you, making your ritual space into a sphere.

Face the east and say:

> *I call upon the powers of air.*
> *Join me in this rite.*
> *I call upon the powers of communication, clarity, wisdom, and song.*
> *Join my circle and bring your energy.*
> *Hail and welcome air.*

Face the south and say:

> *I call upon the powers of fire.*
> *Join me in this rite.*
> *I call upon the powers of heat, passion, creativity, and power.*
> *Join my circle and bring your energy.*
> *Hail and welcome fire.*

Face the west and say:

> *I call upon the powers of water.*
> *Join me in this rite.*
> *I call upon the powers of intuition, emotion, depth, and knowing.*

Join my circle and bring your energy.
Hail and welcome water.

Face the north and say:

I call upon the powers of earth.
Join me in this rite.
I call upon the powers of strength, stability, craft, and skill.
Join my circle and bring your energy.
Hail and welcome earth.

If you are invoking deity into your ritual, this is the time to do so.

Step up to your altar. Light the incense and say: "With the blessing of air."

Light the candle and say: "With the blessing of fire."

Hold up the first bowl of water and say: "With the blessing of water."

Hold up the bowl of soil and say: "With the blessing of earth."

Place three pinches of salt into the second bowl of water. Say: "With the blessings of salt and the blessings of water combined, a sacred being is formed."

Sprinkle this water over your tool. Say: "This tool is cleansed of the mundane. It will now take its position as a tool of the sacred artes."

Run the tool through the smoke of the incense. Say: "I charge this tool with the power of air, to know, communication, clarity. I charge this tool in the sacred arte."

Hold the tool up to the sky.

Run the tool through the flame of the candle. Say: "I charge this tool with the power of fire, to will, passion, creativity. I charge this tool in the sacred arte."

Hold the tool up to the sky.

Place the tool in the non-salted bowl of water or sprinkle that water over the tool. Say: "I charge this tool with the power of water, to dare, intuition, emotion. I charge this tool in the sacred arte."

Hold the tool up to the sky.

Place the tool in the bowl of soil or sprinkle the soil over the tool. Say:

I charge this tool with the power of earth, to keep silent, stability, skill.
I charge this tool in the sacred arte.

Hold the tool up to the sky.

If you have called deity into your circle, this is the time to ask for their blessing. Speak out loud and from the heart.

Place the tool in your upturned palms and say:

I charge and consecrate this tool with the power of the elements.
That which is made sacred cannot be unmade.
With the blessings of the Mighty Ones and the powers of the four corners,
this tool is consecrated and sacred.
Blessed be.

Set the tool back in the center of your altar space. If you have more tools to consecrate, do this now, one tool at a time. When you are finished with all the tools, begin closing your ritual space.

If you have invoked deity, now is the time to speak your thanks and release them from the ritual space.

Face the north and say:

All hail the powers of earth.
Thank you for joining me in this rite.
Hail and farewell earth.

Face the east and say:

All hail the powers of air.
Thank you for joining me in this rite.
Hail and farewell air.

Face the south and say:

All hail the powers of fire.
Thank you for joining me in this rite.
Hail and farewell fire.

Face the west and say:

> *All hail the powers of water.*
> *Thank you for joining me in this rite.*
> *Hail and farewell water.*

Using the two fingers of your dominant hand, release the above and below of your circle and then pull back the energy of the circle you built, releasing its power.

The rite is done. Store your tool wrapped in black fabric and keep it closed away for one full moon cycle before you officially begin using it in ceremonies.

Supplies for Ritual

Beyond the ceremonial tools you might use in ritual, there are other tools that could also be considered correspondences that can help the flow and efficacy of your magickal workings.

PLANTS

Greenbloods, also known as plants, have been magickal allies since there has been awareness of magick. Different plants carry different energetic signatures and can help boost the energy and focus of the ceremonies you create. Plants can be burned as incense or for other smoke fumigation uses. They can be added to baths and magickal washes. They can be made into teas, added to oils, and used in charms and mojo bags. They can also be used for decorative purposes.

There are excellent books available that speak to the magickal uses of plants in rituals, ceremonies, and spells. One that I highly recommend was written by Scott Cunningham, and it's called *Cunningham's Encyclopedia of Magical Herbs*.

Herbs and Flowers

Herbs can be used in rituals in lots of different ways. You might burn them as incense, use them in spell ingredients, or add them to oils and other potions.

Fresh herbs, dried herbs, and powdered herbs can all work in a pinch. However, whether they are fresh, dried, or powered can increase or decrease their medicinal usages and could impact their magickal uses. Make sure you do your research.

The same is true for flowers. They can be used in all the same ways as herbs, but be aware that many flowers are not safe for consumption, so be careful with what you use. Flowers are also a common decoration for ritual altars. Selecting flowers that match the energy of the ceremony about to take place is an added touch of magick.

Purchasing herbs online is always a fine option, just make sure you are ordering from a reputable company. Unfortunately, there are a lot of charlatans willing to sell you cheap herbs as a replacement for something more exotic or expensive, thinking you won't know the difference.

The herbs included in the following chart are herbs that are easier to access. Some herbs are more obscure and harder to obtain or are really expensive. If you don't have a local herb or natural food store, you might not be able to procure some of the less-common herbs. The herbs on this list could be found in the grocery store produce section, in the tea section, or in the bottles of dried cooking herbs. Some you might even be able to find growing wild around where you live!

Wildcrafting is the practice of gathering herbs from the world around you where they are naturally growing, typically wild places. But this could also be parks, neighborhood yards, in the cracks of the pavement, and so on. When it comes to wildcrafting, be sure you are 100 percent certain of the identification of a plant before you use it or consume it.

Plant	Element	Planet(s)	Zodiac Sign(s)	Day of the Week	Direction	Main Energy
Agrimony	Air	Jupiter	Cancer		East	Protection
Allspice	Fire	Mars	Aries, Scorpio	Tuesday	South	Prosperity
Aloe	Water	Moon	Cancer, Libra		West	Protection
Angelica	Fire	Sun	Aries, Leo		South	Power
Anise	Air	Jupiter	Aquarius, Gemini		East	Protection
Basil	Fire	Mars	Aries, Scorpio	Tuesday	South	Love
Bergamot	Air	Mercury	Gemini, Virgo		East	Abundance
Blackberry	Water	Venus	Aries, Scorpio		West	Protection
Black Cohosh	Fire	Mars			South	Protection
Borage	Air	Jupiter	Leo		East	Abundance
Broom	Air	Mars	Aries		East	Banishing
Cardamom	Water	Venus	Taurus		West	Love
Carnation	Fire	Sun	Aries, Capricorn	Sunday	South	Healing
Catnip	Water	Venus	Libra, Pisces		West	Love
Chamomile	Water	Sun	Leo	Monday		Banishing

Plant	Element	Planet(s)	Zodiac Sign(s)	Day of the Week	Direction	Main Energy
Cinnamon	Fire	Sun	Aries, Capricorn	Thursday	South	Love
Clove	Fire	Jupiter	Aries, Leo		South	Prosperity
Comfrey	Water	Saturn	Capricorn		West	Prosperity
Coriander	Fire	Mars	Aries		South	Love
Cumin	Fire	Mars	Aries, Scorpio		South	Protection
Daffodil	Water	Venus	Leo, Sagittarius		West	Luck
Daisy	Water	Venus	Taurus		West	Love
Dandelion	Air	Jupiter	Aquarius, Libra		East	Clairvoyance
Dill	Fire	Mercury	Cancer, Gemini	Wednesday	South	Protection
Fennel	Fire	Mercury	Aries, Gemini		South	Healing
Frankincense	Fire	Sun	Aquarius, Aries	Sunday	South	Protection
Garlic	Fire	Mars	Aries	Tuesday	South	Banishing
Geranium	Water	Venus	Aries, Cancer		West	Healing
Ginger	Fire	Mars	Aries, Sagittarius	Tuesday	South	Love
Ginseng	Fire	Sun			South	Healing

Plant	Element	Planet(s)	Zodiac Sign(s)	Day of the Week	Direction	Main Energy
Hyssop	Fire	Jupiter		Sunday	East	Banishing
Jasmine	Water	Moon	Cancer, Capricorn	Monday, Wednesday	West	Prosperity
Lavender	Air	Mercury	Aquarius, Gemini	Wednesday	East	Peace
Lemon Balm	Water	Jupiter, moon	Cancer		West	Clarity
Marigold	Fire	Sun	Cancer, Leo	Sunday	South	Clairvoyance
Marjoram	Air	Mercury	Aries, Gemini		East	Prosperity
Mugwort	Earth	Venus	Cancer, Gemini		North	Clairvoyance
Mullein	Fire	Saturn	Libra	Saturday	South	Protection
Mustard	Fire	Mars	Aries		South	Protection
Myrrh	Water	Moon	Aquarius, Cancer	Saturday	West	Healing
Nettle	Fire	Mars	Aries, Scorpio		South	Banishing
Nutmeg	Fire	Jupiter	Leo, Pisces	Thursday	South	Luck
Patchouli	Earth	Saturn	Pisces		North	Prosperity
Pepper	Fire	Mars	Aries		South	Protection
Peppermint	Fire	Mercury	Aquarius, Aries		South	Healing

Plant	Element	Planet(s)	Zodiac Sign(s)	Day of the Week	Direction	Main Energy
Raspberry	Water	Venus	Leo, Taurus	Friday	West	Protection
Rose	Water	Venus	Cancer, Libra	Friday	West	Love
Rosemary	Fire	Sun	Aquarius, Aries		South	Protection
Sage	Air	Jupiter	Aquarius, Pisces	Thursday	East	Protection
Snapdragon	Fire	Mars	Gemini	Tuesday	South	Protection
Spearmint	Water	Venus	Libra		West	Healing
Star Anise	Air	Jupiter	Pisces, Sagittarius		East	Clairvoyance
Strawberry	Water	Venus	Libra	Friday	West	Love
Sunflower	Fire	Sun	Leo	Sunday	South	Healing
Thistle	Fire	Mars	Scorpio	Tuesday	South	Banishing
Thyme	Water	Venus	Aries, Capricorn	Saturday	West	Clairvoyance
Valerian	Water	Venus	Scorpio, Virgo		West	Love
Vanilla	Water	Venus	Libra, Scorpio		West	Love
Yarrow	Water	Venus	Gemini		West	Clairvoyance

Trees

Trees have been held as sacred in many, if not most, cultures around the world. Some ancient traditions would hold their rites and rituals in a grove of trees. Trees provide us with food and shelter, as well as the very air we breathe. Trees also provide the wood for ritual tools and sacred fires.

Just like other greenbloods, different trees hold different energetics. Choosing the right kind of wood for a magickal tool or as part of your spell or ceremony can add to the flow and energy you want to create.

The following list of trees and woods is a very generic list. These types of trees are found in many places. However, it is good to learn the specific types of these trees and how they might impact your working. There are also local trees that only grow where you live. Learn about these trees, both from a magickal and mundane perspective, connect with these trees, and add them to your rituals as a way to honor the land you live on.

Plant	Element(s)	Planet(s)	Zodiac Sign(s)	Day(s) of the Week	Direction	Main Energy
Alder	Air, fire	Mars, Venus	Aries, Cancer	Saturday		Protection
Apple	Water	Venus	Aquarius, Cancer	Friday	West	Love
Ash	Fire, water	Sun	Aquarius, Pisces	Sunday		Protection
Birch	Water	Venus	Capricorn, Sagittarius	Monday, Sunday		Banishing
Cedar	Fire	Sun	Aries, Sagittarius	Tuesday	South	Protection
Cherry	Water	Venus	Aquarius, Aries			Love
Chestnut	Fire	Jupiter	Cancer, Gemini			Love
Cypress	Earth	Saturn	Aquarius, Capricorn	Saturday	West	Healing
Elder	Water	Venus	Capricorn, Sagittarius	Monday	West	Banishing
Elm	Water	Saturn	Capricorn, Sagittarius	Tuesday		Love
Fir	Air	Jupiter, Mars	Aries			Prosperity
Hazel	Air	Sun	Gemini, Leo	Wednesday		Protection
Holly	Fire	Mars	Aries, Cancer	Tuesday	South	Protection
Juniper	Fire	Sun	Aries, Leo		South	Protection
Laurel	Air, fire	Sun	Gemini, Leo	Thursday, Sunday		Banishing

Plant	Element(s)	Planet(s)	Zodiac Sign(s)	Day(s) of the Week	Direction	Main Energy
Maple	Air	Jupiter	Cancer, Libra	Thursday		Abundance
Myrtle	Water	Venus	Sagittarius	Friday, Monday		Love
Oak	Fire	Sun	Cancer, Gemini	Thursday		Abundance
Olive	Fire	Sun	Aquarius, Aries			Healing
Pine	Air	Mars	Aquarius, Aries	Thursday	East	Banishing
Poplar	Water	Saturn				Clairvoyance
Rowan	Fire	Sun	Capricorn, Sagittarius	Wednesday		Clairvoyance
Spruce	Earth, water	Jupiter, Venus	Cancer, Capricorn			Prosperity
Sycamore	Air, water					Abundance
Walnut	Fire	Sun	Leo, Virgo			Healing
Willow	Water	Moon	Pisces, Taurus	Monday		Love
Yew	Water	Saturn	Capricorn			Other Realms

CHARMS, AMULETS, AND TALISMANS

When it comes right down to it, a charm, an amulet, and a talisman aren't all that different from each other. They are all types of spells, and they are typically created in ritual space. However, their origination and use vary slightly from each other. Although they are slightly different processes, most modern Witches use these three terms interchangeably.

Charms, amulets, and talismans can all be made from items that are plant-based or animal-based. They could be handcrafted by you or another person. These items might be jewelry that you have imbued with specific powers, or they could be coins, trinkets, or any number of other things.

Using or working magick with these types of objects is not required to practice Witchcraft. You might love the idea of using animal parts for your charms, talismans, and amulets. You might be totally against using animal parts in your charms. And/or you might want to make sure that any animal parts you use are ethically sourced. All of these responses and reactions are totally okay. Only you get to determine what is best for your practice.

Also know that some animal parts are illegal to buy, sell, or even possess. Make sure that you check the laws where you live and follow the rules of what is legal and allowed.

Charms (Luck)

The word *charm* originally referred to a magickal song or chant that was used for enchantment. The root of the word is *charme*, which is a French word that means song.[21] However, from a modern perspective, a charm and a song are no longer the same thing. For most modern Witches, a charm is an object that brings good luck.

Anything can be made into a charm, but most often they are small objects that can fit in a pocket or be worn or hidden easily.

There are some charms that have made their way into popular culture; horseshoes, four-leaf clovers, buttons, and charm bracelets are all types of

---

21   Online Etymology Dictionary, s.v. "charm (n.)," updated December 5, 2018, https://www .etymonline.com/word/charm.

charms that people use or have in their everyday lives without realizing they are interacting with magick.

Amulets (Protection)

An amulet is a more ancient form of a charm. Amulets were worn or hung in homes to protect family, livestock, and structures. Use of the word *amulet* can be traced back to Pliny the Elder, who wrote that they were used for exorcistic and therapeutic benefits.[22] They were made from different metals with specific symbols carved into them to bestow the wearer with protection or other magickal powers.

Amulets are typically worn on the body and not taken off.

Common protection amulets you might have seen out in the world are evil eyes, bells, skeleton keys, garlic, and cords with knots.

Talismans (Giving Power)

Where an amulet is a protective type of charm, a talisman is a magickal object that will imbue the user with power. An example is wearing an eagle claw for insight and strength. A talisman is going to give the wearer something beyond their regular power.

Typically, these are worn on the body, but they may also be placed strategically close to where the person might need that energy the most.

Animal parts and bones are often used as talismans, as well as pentacles, specifically created sigils, and so on.

Types of Charms/Amulets/Talismans
+ **Acorn:** Fertility, abundance.
+ **Alligator Foot:** Wealth, money.
+ **Ankh:** Spiritual pursuits, Underworld communication.
+ **Bay Leaf:** Protection, keeping rites hidden.
+ **Bells:** Clear negative energy, keep the Fae away.
+ **Buckeye:** Protection, money.
+ **Buffalo Tooth:** Strength, power.

---

22   Thwaite, "A History of Amulets in Ten Objects."

+ **Butterfly Wing:** Transformation, change.
+ **Button:** Luck, ancestors.
+ **Cat Claw:** Protection, hexing.
+ **Clove:** Seeking love, seeking sex.
+ **Crab Claw:** Seeking love, fertility.
+ **Deer Antler:** Fertility, success.
+ **Elk Tooth:** Vitality, strength.
+ **Evil Eye:** Protection, clearing negativity.
+ **Four-Leaf Clover:** Luck, money.
+ **Foxtail:** Cleverness, quickness.
+ **Garlic Clove:** Protection, clearing evil.
+ **Horn:** Virility, wealth.
+ **Horseshoe:** Good luck, protection.
+ **Knotted Cords:** Trapping spirits, specific spell workings.
+ **Nutmeg:** Luck, gambling.
+ **Pine Cone:** Health, healing.
+ **Rabbit Foot:** Good luck, wealth.
+ **Racoon Penis Bone:** Virility, seeking sex.
+ **Rice:** Fertility, money.
+ **Scarab:** Clearing evil, Underworld communication.
+ **Scorpion:** Protection, hexing.
+ **Skeleton Keys:** Unlocking stuck situations, crossroads magick.
+ **Snake Shed:** Transformation, change.
+ **Tonka Beans:** Good luck, money.
+ **Turtle Shell:** Protection, home magick.
+ **Wishbone:** Wishes, good luck.

Oil and Incense Formulas

Oils and incense can really add to your rituals. Scent is such a powerful sense. Certain scents can calm us, excite us, and bring back memories. Creating your own oils and incense blends is one of the most fun parts of Witchcraft. Getting in there, making potions, and getting your hands a bit dirty is all part of the magick.

OILS

Ritual oils are blends of essential oils that are put into a carrier oil. Essential oils are too concentrated to be used on their own; they must be diluted with a carrier oil. Carrier oils can be virtually any oil you want, but some are better than others. Oils like jojoba oil, almond oil, apricot kernel oil, and grapeseed oil are all bland with little scent, so they won't interfere with your essential oils.

When making an oil, mix the essential oils together first, then add your blend to the carrier oil. Each of the following recipes should be diluted in two ounces of carrier oil. You can adjust the essential oil formulas if you determine you want to make more or less of any of these blends.

Some of the suggested essential oils are either hard to come by or very expensive. It's totally okay to use a synthetic alternative, as long as you don't have an allergic reaction.

Abundance Oil

- 5 drops bergamot
- 3 drops ginger
- 1 drop patchouli
- 2 oz carrier oil

Anointing Oil

- 3 drops clove
- 3 drops cinnamon
- 2 drops myrrh
- 1 drop sandalwood
- 1 drop sweet orange
- 2 oz carrier oil

Love Oil

- 5 drops rose
- 3 drops cinnamon
- 3 drops neroli
- 2 oz carrier oil

Protection Oil

+ 3 drops black pepper
+ 3 drops basil
+ 3 drops cedar
+ 2 oz carrier oil

INCENSE

Incenses can be powdered, formed into sticks or cones, or blended dried herbs that are burned on a charcoal. Herbs don't smell the same when you compare the fresh, dried, and burning. It might take some time and practice to get your formulas right.

Most incense bases are made up from a mixture of wood pulp or shavings, charcoal powders, gum arabic, and sodium nitrate or potassium nitrate. This combination helps the incense bind together and burn continuously. You can make a great incense base without either of the nitrates, but your incense will need a charcoal disk to burn.

Drops of oil can also be added to incense mixtures. This will also slightly change the scent of the incense while it is burning. Oil tends to add a more intense odor to an incense base. Make sure you don't add too much, otherwise the base will be too wet and it won't burn.

The following formulas are considered noncombustible forms of incense that include dried herbs, some seeds, and resins. These will need to be burned on top of a charcoal incense burner. It is best to pulverize the ingredients as much as possible to try and get a fine powder. Using a mortar and pestle is best because it requires you to grind by hand and you can set your intention into the incense. However, if this is too challenging, an electric coffee or herb grinder will work too.

These formulas can either be made with a wood incense base or as a standalone incense. If you decide to include a wood incense base in your mixture, add one part wood to all the other ingredients combined.

Cleansing Incense

- ◆ 1 part benzoin resin
- ◆ 1 part white copal resin
- ◆ 2 parts dried rosemary
- ◆ 2 parts dried dill
- ◆ Finely ground salt

Drawing Down Incense

- ◆ 2 parts dried gardenia leaves
- ◆ 2 parts dried rose petals
- ◆ 2 parts dried basil
- ◆ 1 star anise

Grounding Incense

- ◆ 2 parts pine needles
- ◆ 2 parts cedar
- ◆ 1 part dried mint

Protection Incense

- ◆ 2 parts dragon's blood resin
- ◆ 1 part angelica root
- ◆ 1 clove

Ritual Incense

- ◆ 2 parts dried rose petals
- ◆ 2 parts cedar
- ◆ 1 part frankincense resin
- ◆ 1 part dried rosemary
- ◆ 1 bay leaf

Step One: Cleansing Body and Spirit

The first step for any ritual should be a spiritual cleanse. A spiritual cleanse is simply a practice of keeping good spiritual hygiene. Most cleansings are really easy exercises that help you prepare to step into ritual space. By cleansing, you get yourself ready and presentable from a spiritual perspective.

Cleansing isn't a practice that is unique to Witchcraft. Most spiritual cultures across the planet have some type of cleansing practice, ranging from private to communal:

*   Every April in Thailand they have the Songkran Festival. This is a three-day event where homes are given a deep cleaning, old items are burned, and devotional statues are washed. The water from the washed statues is collected and then a water fight ensues.[23] Fun! The water is considered a blessing for abundance in the coming year.
*   Every spring equinox in Persia they celebrate Nowruz. It is a huge spring cleansing, where old and broken items are gotten rid of, rugs are beaten, and homes are deep cleaned.[24]
*   The concept of cleansing with smoke can be found all over the world. A smoke cleanse is the process of burning certain herbs and using the smoke to cleanse the spirit body. There is a range of specific herbs used, depending on the part of the world. In the Celtic diaspora, a smoke cleansing practice is called *saining*. In some cultures it is called a *havan*. Several Native tribes call this practice *smudging*.
*   In Finland, going into the sauna and sweating detoxifies the body and cleanses the spirit. It is a deeply cultural and spiritual practice that is still maintained today. There is even a sauna spirit that resides in every sauna and must be honored.[25]
*   In Mexico, Central America, and South America, there is a cleansing practice called *limpia*. In this practice, a large bundle of herbs is beaten all over the body in order to cleanse the person

---

23   Benjamin, "Cleaning and Renewal Rituals from Around the World."
24   Benjamin, "Cleaning and Renewal Rituals from Around the World."
25   "Spirit of the Sauna."

of negative energy. This is often performed in conjunction with an egg cleanse and/or alcohol being sprayed over the head of the individual being cleansed.[26]

There are a ton of different cultural ways to cleanse. Some of these have made their way into modern Witchcraft practices.

BATH CLEANSING

Bathing can be a spiritual practice. A cleansing bath can be done with salts, herbs, and/or oils added to the bathwater. Salt is a great neutralizer that helps shift negative energy by absorbing it out of your body. If you choose to add herbs or oils, pick ones that have a spiritual relationship with cleansing. Here are some of my favorite cleansing bath ingredients:

+ Sea salt
+ Vinegar
+ Hyssop
+ Sage
+ Rosemary
+ Lemongrass
+ Bay leaf
+ Rue
+ Cedar

Bath Cleansing Practice #1

For this cleansing, you will need the following:

+ 1 tablespoon dried hyssop
+ 1 tablespoon dried lemongrass
+ 1 tablespoon dried cedar
+ 1 cup sea salt
+ Small pot of water
+ Bathtub

---

26   Glenn, "Limpias – Energetic and Spiritual Cleansing."

Place all of the herbs in a small pot of water and bring that water to a boil. Allow the water to cool until it is safe to touch.

As the water is cooling, fill up your bathtub and add in the sea salt.

Once the herb water has cooled, strain it and add the herb infused water to the bath. Discard the herbs.

Get in and soak.

Bath Cleansing Practice #2

For this cleansing, you will need the following:

- 1 tablespoon sea salt
- 1 cup apple cider vinegar
- Bathtub

Fill up the bathtub with warm water. As the bath fills, add in the sea salt so it has time to fully dissolve. Once the tub is full, add the apple cider vinegar.

Get in and soak.

SMOKE CLEANSE/FUMIGATION

A smoke cleanse is exactly what it sounds like: you use the smoke from burning herbs or resins to cleanse your spirit body. Point of clarity here—this is to cleanse your *spirit* body, not your physical body. Don't put burning herbs on your skin!

If you have any breathing issues, lung damage, or asthma, smoke cleansing may not be the best choice for you. Check with your doctor first.

Don't use a smoke cleanse in a small, tight, or unventilated space. Some herbs and resins will smoke more than others and you might find smoke alarms going off if you're not careful.

Some herbs, and especially resins, won't burn well, if at all, without a consistent heat source. An incense charcoal disk will work when in this situation. All of the herbs that are good for a bath cleanse are also appropriate for a smoke cleanse.

Here are some resins that are excellent for smoke cleansing:

+ Dragon's blood
+ Frankincense
+ Myrrh
+ White copal
+ Black copal
+ Benzoin

Smoke Cleansing Practice #1

For this cleansing, you will need the following:

+ Long dried sprigs of rosemary
+ Long dried stalks of lavender
+ Long dried pieces of cedar
+ Thin, plain, natural twine cording
+ Lighter
+ Firesafe plate or bowl

Ideally, perform this action outside. Wrap all the dried herbs with the twine so you have a tight bundle. Light one side of the bundle and hold it over the firesafe container. Hold the smoking bundle and move it around your body, remembering to get the back of your body with the smoke too.

When the process feels complete, grind out the burning herbs in the firesafe container. If you are uncertain the fire is totally out, douse it with water. The herb bundle can be saved and used again.

Smoke Cleansing Practice #2

For this cleansing, you will need the following:

+ Fire- and heat-safe container
+ Incense charcoal
+ Lighter
+ Large pinch of white copal resin
+ Large pinch of benzoin resin
+ Large pinch of frankincense resin

Light the charcoal in your firesafe container until it is hot. Place the resins on top of the disk. Use this smoke to cleanse your body or the physical location where a ritual is about to take place.

DRUMMING/RATTLING

A drum or rattle can break up stuck energy around your body and in your etheric body. This type of cleanse is best done with a partner, as it is really difficult to drum or rattle completely around your own body. With this type of cleanse, it is especially important to pay attention to the spine.

Rattle Cleansing Practice

For this cleansing, you will need the following:

+ Rattle
+ Friend/covenmate/partner

One person takes the rattle and the other person stands with their legs apart and arms open.

The individual with the rattle should begin by standing in front of the other person. Start shaking the rattle at the top of the head, moving slowly down and around the front of the body. Once that is complete, move around to the back, starting at the feet and slowly moving upward, shaking the rattle from the feet back to the top of the head.

Switch roles.

BREATHWORK

Learning to control and focus your breath is a powerful spiritual practice used by cultures all over the world. Having a solid breathing practice can calm you down, shift your energy, bring peace, lessen anxiety, and cleanse your spirit body.

Breathwork Cleansing Practice

For this cleansing, you will need the following:

+ Five minutes of uninterrupted time

Sit in a place where you can be comfortable and undisturbed for at least five minutes. Sit with your spine as straight as possible, with your arms relaxed and your palms facing up.

Breathe in through your nose to the count of four.

Pause for the count of two.

Exhale through your mouth to the count of eight.

Pause for the count of two.

Repeat for at least five minutes.

ENERGY CLEANSE

An energy cleanse requires you to work with your spirit body or auric field. Scan your body, taking time to notice any areas that feel stuck, dark, or torn. Typically, energy cleanses utilize calling earth energy up into your body to clear any stuck negative energy. If this is unfamiliar or uncomfortable, seek out a professional energy healer who can utilize their healing energy to help clear out anything stuck or negative.

Energy Cleansing Practice

For this cleansing, you will need the following:

◆ Five minutes of uninterrupted time

Stand with your legs apart and your spine straight.

Breathe deeply and give yourself time to scan your body. Let your awareness move up and across your body. If you notice an area that feels weak or fuzzy, breathe up from the earth. Visualize drawing energy up from the earth and into your body like a glowing, healing light. Send it to the part of you that feels out of sorts; focus your breath in that area. Continue to do this until you feel stronger and your energy is clear.

ESPURGING

The process of espurging is done with holy water, blessed water, or salted water and herbs. Ideally, dried herbs with long stems are used as a vehicle to sprinkle the salted water. You can also add herbs to a holy water base.

Holy water can be purchased online or from spiritual retailers. If you're feeling particularly brave, you could also go to a local Catholic church and ask for holy water. Some churches are more likely to oblige than others. If seeking out Catholic holy water doesn't feel like something you want to incorporate into your practice, you can always make your own holy water.

The following spellwork for making holy water is inspired by the process laid out in *Psychic Self-Defense* by Dion Fortune.[27]

Making Holy Water

To make holy water, you will need the following:

+ A medium-sized glass bowl
+ Your ritual knife or athame
+ Kosher salt in a small bowl
+ Water in a small bowl

Start by placing the tip of your athame in the bowl of salt. Say:

> *I exorcise thee, creature of earth, by the living divine and my own holiness.*
> *Oh creature of earth, be clean.*
> *In the name of the living divine and my own holiness.*
> *Blessed be.*

Next, put the tip of your athame into the bowl of water. Say:

> *I exorcise thee, creature of water, by the living divine and my own holiness.*
> *Oh creature of water, be clean.*
> *In the name of the living divine and my own holiness.*
> *Blessed be.*

Pour the water into your glass bowl. Slowly sprinkle in the blessed salt and say:

> *I bless this salt to bring forth health from the body.*
> *I bless this salt to bring forth health from the soul.*

---

27   Fortune, *Psychic Self Defense*, 188–89.

Using the first two fingers of your dominant hand, draw a pentacle over the top of the glass bowl.

The water can then be used in ritual or poured into a bottle for safe-keeping. This water will only be good for a couple of weeks.

Espurging Cleansing Practice

For this cleansing, you will need the following:

- Long, loose branches of bay laurel
- Large bowl of salted water
- Friend/covenmate/partner

One partner stands with their legs wide and arms open. The other partner dips the branches of the laurel into the bowl of salted water and sprinkles that over the top of the head. The branches may also be lightly smacked against the skin. The branches may need to be frequently dipped into the salt water throughout the process.

When complete, switch roles.

COLOGNE/ALCOHOL/WATER CLEANSE

In many traditions, the use of alcohol or cologne is part of a spiritual cleansing of the body, is used to ground, or is used to clear ritual space. These same colognes or spirits might also be used as offerings for deities or entities being called into the ritual. You may have seen or attended rituals where alcohol, spirits, or cologne were spat across the ritual space. This is done to cleanse the space and make it ready for ritual. Some examples of spiritual colognes are:

- Rum
- Florida water
- Hoyt's Cologne
- Orange blossom water
- Rosewater

Cologne Cleansing Practice

For this cleansing, you will need the following:

- Bottle of Florida water

Pour a dime-sized amount of Florida water into the palm of your hands.

Rub the water into your palms and then run your hands from your forehead across to the back of your head.

Place your hands on the top of your head and breathe in deeply.

Move your hands from the front of your head to the back of your head again, and then slide your hands across the back of your neck.

Clap three times.

EGG CLEANSE

Using an egg to cleanse your spirit body is a folk magick practice done by many different cultures across the globe. This cleansing practice is best done with the help of another person.

The process works by rolling an egg down the body. The idea is the egg absorbs any negative energy from the body. In some traditions, you would then crack the egg open to determine if the cleansing was successful and divine any other actions that might need to be taken. In other traditions, the eggs used for cleansing must be immediately discarded or tossed into running water.

Egg Cleansing Practice

For this cleansing, you will need the following:

- At least one egg per person
- Friend/covenmate/partner
- A body of water

One partner stands with their spine straight, legs wide, and arms apart. The other partner takes the egg and, starting in the front of the body, at the top of their partner's head, rolls the egg down the body from head to foot, repeating this on the other leg and then both arms. This process should be repeated along the back of the body as well. If the egg is dropped or breaks, the process must start completely over.

Once complete, the partners switch roles and a new egg is used.

Afterward, the used eggs should be taken to a body of water and released.

FASTING

Abstaining from drugs, alcohol, food, or electronic entertainment are all ways to participate in a fast and cleanse yourself before a ritual.

Fasting Cleansing Practice

This fasting requires several days of prep.

Don't imbibe any drugs or alcohol for at least a week prior to your ritual working. At least forty-eight hours before the ritual, stop the use of all electronics—this means phones, television, and computers.

If you want to try advanced-level fasting, stop all solid food at least twenty-four hours before the ritual is set to start. Only perform this practice if you have been cleared by a medical professional.

After the ritual is complete, don't just jump back in. Give yourself time to slowly reincorporate these things back into your life.

ANOINTING

Although not a specific cleansing practice, using anointing oils after a cleanse is an excellent way to shift your energy into a ritual headspace. Ceremonial oils can be purchased or made by you in ritual space. The scent of an anointing oil should be appealing to you and help you feel spiritually shifted. Scent is a powerful sense; it can bring up memories and emotions. Use that to your magickal advantage.

I have two ritual oils that I use regularly. One is what I call my "Priestex ritual oil" and it is a blend that I wear when I am holding a ritual role and want to feel connected to the ancestors of the Craft. The other is a psychic oil that I place upon my Witch's eye (or third eye) before doing tarot card readings.

You can anoint yourself before rituals to help you enter the right frame of mind for the rite you are performing. You can anoint yourself during ritual as part of the ritual flow or the magickal working. You can anoint yourself after ritual as a way of grounding and coming fully back into your body and the mundane.

Anointing oils can be used on candles, mojo bags, or other spell pieces. They can also be used on statues or images of deities that you work with as a sign of your devotion.

Step Two: Grounding and Centering

Once you have done the work of cleansing your spirit body externally, the next step is to shift your internal focus and bring your emotional body fully present. It is vital to the success of a ritual for you to be present, which is easier said than done sometimes.

Grounding helps you to shake off distractions and be in the moment. It also helps you remember your connection to the earth and feel your threads of connection with the planet. During ritual you can (and should) utilize earth energy by pulling it up and into your body. If you use all your own energy during a ritual, you might be left feeling a bit hungover or depleted.

There are many ways to ground and center yourself. Some practices may be easier for you than others.

TREE OF LIFE GROUNDING

The Tree of Life grounding process is one that will be familiar for most modern Witchcraft practitioners. Variations of this exercise are often done at the beginning of rituals and public gatherings.

✦ **Exercise** ✦

Stand or sit with your spine as straight as possible. Close your eyes and connect with your body. Breathe deeply and with the intention to be firmly rooted in your body. As you breathe, send tendrils of your spiritual roots out from the bottoms of your feet into the earth below you. With each breath, let the roots sink down deeper and deeper. Allow your roots to go down, down, down, deeper into the earth.

When you feel ready, as you exhale, send down any energy that doesn't serve you or this ritual through your roots and into the earth, where it can be composted. Release anything you don't need at this moment.

Then, when you feel ready, breathe in the energy of the earth. With each inhale allow the earth energy to travel up your roots, flowing up, up, up, until that energy reaches the bottom of your feet.

The energy of the earth continues to move upward, filling your feet and your ankles. The earth energy moves up your calves and shins, filling your body and cells with grounding earth energy.

With each inhale, that energy continues to move up into your thighs, then fills your pelvic bowl. The earth energy flows up your spine and your belly, flows up your rib cage, filling you with the power of the earth. The earth energy flows around your shoulders, down your arms, and out your fingertips.

The energy flows up and around your neck, around the back of your skull, and swirls around your jaw. The energy of the earth flows around your cheeks, temples, and forehead. Finally, it comes to a close at the top of your head.

From there, the energy rains out from the top of your head like a fountain, right out of your crown. It showers around you, clearing out the energy of your auric body, allowing you to be fully present in this moment, right now.

Breathe deeply. When you feel ready, open your eyes and be here now.

ROOTS DOWN, BRANCHES UP

This is a variation of the Tree of Life grounding process. Once you are comfortable with the Tree of Life, the Roots Down, Branches Up exercise is a much faster tool. This grounding practice is good when you have a short time to ground or when you are stepping into a situation that could be stressful or emotionally challenging.

✦ Exercise ✦

Stand or sit with your spine as straight as possible. Breathe deeply and with the intention to connect with your body. Take three large, deep breaths. On the last exhale, shoot your roots down into the earth, having them reach as deep into the earth as possible.

When you feel ready, take three large, deep breaths. On the last exhale, shoot some branches up into the sky. Allow them to extend into the sky as far as they can go.

Allow yourself to be connected to the three realms: in the earth, on the earth, and above the earth. Be the kiss between earth and heaven. Feel the flow of earth and sky with you as the conduit. Allow this to clear you, cleanse you, and bring you into focused awareness.

When you are ready, call your branches back into your body and take a deep breath. When you are ready, call your roots back into your body and take a deep breath. Let yourself be here now.

CALLING BACK YOUR THREADS

One of the issues that keeps us from being fully present is outside distraction. It could be our work, the cat food we need to pick up from the store, or the fight we had with our partner. We could be distracted by a late bill looming over our heads or what needs to be made for dinner. The Calling Back Your Threads grounding practice helps you bring all your parts and pieces back into your body so you can be fully present.

✦ Exercise ✦

Stand or sit with your spine as straight as possible. Close your eyes and breathe deeply. Feel the edges of your body.

As you breathe, scan your body, looking for any areas where you feel your energy is being pulled away, tugged, or tightened. When you find one of these places, simply pull the energy back. Imagine you can just reel that energy back to you, as if it was a fishing line.

Continue to scan your body, looking for areas that are pulled away or stretched away from you. Any time you find one of these places, reel the energy back into your body, calling all of yourself back to your center.

When you feel complete, do one final scan to make sure you haven't missed anything. Finally, take a deep breath, open your eyes, and be here now.

Step Three: Creating the Boundary

In most Witchcraft traditions, there is a process of creating sacred space. First of all, let's be really clear: we silly humans aren't "creating" anything. The land, the space, the world, is already sacred. It is human hubris to think that anything we do makes space sacred.

However, the phrase *creating sacred space* is one that most practitioners of Witchcraft will be familiar with, so that is the term we will use for the purposes of this book. Creating sacred space is simply a moment of recognition that we are moving from mundane thoughts into magickal ones.

We go through the process of creating sacred space for multiple reasons. One of the most important reasons is to delineate our mundane lives from our magickal lives. It is a process of shifting our awareness and allowing ourselves to go from our typical state of mind into a more spiritual state of mind.

Another reason for creating sacred space is to make a container for the ritual and magick that we will perform. Inside of sacred space we can allow the ritual to unfold in a steady and focused way. Then, when the time is right, we can release that energy. The process of creating sacred space is like building a cauldron for our magickal potion, the potion being our ritual. Once we determine the time is right, we can tip that cauldron over and pour magick into the universe.

When you have your intention and begin planning out the actual steps of the ritual, all of the pieces of creating sacred space will need to be taken into consideration and should be added to the planning process. The form, style, function, and creation of sacred space should reflect the intention you have already written.

The way that all of these individual pieces are done within ritual may change depending on the type of tradition. Different Witchcraft lineages may have rules or guidelines on how to walk through these steps. If you are working within a specific tradition, follow the rules on how to create sacred space according to the rules of that system. However, if you are a more eclectic practitioner, or a solitary, allow yourself the time and space to play with different options and try out different versions of setting up rites. Just remember to keep your intention in mind.

As mentioned before, the reason for creating a boundary around your ritual space is to hold your ritual's energy in and keep unwanted energies out. Different traditions have different ways of casting the circle or creating the boundary. Some traditions have rules (or implied rules) on which direction you begin to cast your circle, how many circuits of building the circle are required, what words are spoken, and if the elements are invoked at the same time.

The word *circle* is really a misnomer, because what we are creating is a bubble, a sphere of energy to serve as a boundary. In some traditions the size of the circle is very specific; many folks in these traditions will put a marker on the ground, like a chalk or cord circle, in order to trace the energetic boundary in exactly the right place.

Personally, I find these circles to be too small. There is a magickal numerological reason to have a circle be nine or twelve feet, but it can feel restrictive. I was taught that you need to make your boundary big enough so you can move around the ritual space. If casting a circle for a large group event or public ritual, you might want to include the bathrooms in your circle casting. That way every person who needs to use the restroom won't be breaking the boundary every time.

Breaking the boundary happens. People need to leave early; people need to step outside; there are emergencies where someone needs to walk through the edge of the circle. It is best for the person leaving to cut an opening in the boundary, walk through it, and then close up the cut they made once on the other side. This helps hold the structure and integrity of the circle cast.

I was also taught there are two exceptions to the boundary of the circle being broken: children and pets. Pets can come and go in your ritual space, as can small children, and it won't weaken the boundary that you've built. This is because small children and animals are already liminal creatures that see the world differently than we do, and they can cross through liminal spaces without causing disruption.

In the Northern Hemisphere it is common to cast your circle moving in a deosil (or clockwise) direction. In the Southern Hemisphere it is common to cast your circle in a widdershins (or counterclockwise) direction.

Here are a few of my favorite circle-casting techniques.

BLUE FIRE

Using the visualization of Blue Fire is a traditional circle-casting practice used in many modern Witchcraft traditions. I was taught that this type of circle casting uses power called up from the Otherworld, and that power creates a boundary between this world and our ritual. The Blue Fire doesn't belong to any one realm, and all of us can access it.

✦ Exercise ✦

Using a wand, athame, or the first two fingers of your dominant hand, stand in the middle of your ritual space and point your tool to the earth. Call up the power of Blue Fire from the Otherworld. See it, imagine it, visualize it, or act as if there is Blue Fire rising up from the earth and filling your tool.

When you can feel, see, or imagine your tool overflowing with Blue Fire, direct that energy out, facing north and sending it to the edge of your ritual space. Begin to turn in a clockwise direction, allowing the Blue Fire to flow from your tool around your ritual space.

Continue to move in a clockwise circle, returning to the place where you started, all the while sending the Blue Fire from your tool around your circle.

> *When you have completed the circuit, point your tool above you, clos-*
> *ing the top of your circle with Blue Fire. Then point your tool below you,*
> *closing the bottom of your circle with Blue Fire.*
>   *The circle is cast.*

WARDS, WATCHTOWERS, AND PENTACLES

Using pentacles, elementals, and the power of the guardians of the watch-towers to cast a circle is probably one of the most traditional formats of circle casting in modern Witchcraft. This system comes from the Hermetic Order of the Golden Dawn, but it has been connected to many Witchcraft and Wiccan forms of circle casting for decades.

The Order of the Golden Dawn was greatly influenced by older writings about the occult and magick. The biggest inspiration was Enochian magickal lineage, which was born hundreds of years ago in England.[28] Enochian magick calls upon angels that are said to reside, and/or guard, watch-towers located in each of the four classic directions. Two well-known writers about Enochian magick were John Dee and Edward Kelley. The writings of these two, mainly Dee, greatly influenced MacGregor Mathers, who is a forefather of the Hermetic Order of the Golden Dawn.[29]

Using the system of pentacles, elementals, and watchtowers is a pow-erful and effective method of casting a circle. However, if you don't have training or practice working with these energies, this really isn't the ideal—it would be a little like trying to lead a Catholic Mass when you've never been to a Catholic church service. However, learning about these concepts and modifying them to fit your practice and lineage can be a way to con-nect to the old systems while practicing with a powerful modern system that works for you.

The Hermetic Order of the Golden Dawn uses the "quarters" of north, south, east, and west as marking points to cast their energetic circle. The cir-cle is cast by moving in a circle and stopping at each of the directions, or

---

28   Regardie, *The Golden Dawn*, 781–82.
29   Knowles, "S. L. MacGregor Mathers."

quarters/corners, to make a seal, ward, or lock. This is to set the circle and help strengthen the barrier between your sacred space and the outside world.

Most common is the practice of drawing an invoking pentacle in the air in front of you at each of the quarters. This process effectively works like setting a ward, or protective barrier, in each of the directions to protect your circle.

Begin here

Invoking Pentacle

Many traditions take the practice of drawing an invoking pentacle in each corner one step further: they use a different type of invoking pentacle for each of the elements. For example, when facing the east, the specific invoking pentacle for east and air would be used. This adds a level of complexity that is interesting and very ceremonial, but for me, it's too complex of a process and feels unnecessary.

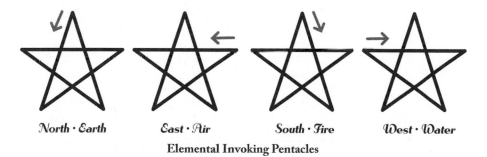

North · Earth   *East · Air*   *South · Fire*   *West · Water*

Elemental Invoking Pentacles

However, your mileage may vary. Try out different ways. Play with different forms of circle casting. See what works best for you.

✦ *Exercise* ✦

Using a wand or athame, stand in the middle of your ritual space. Point your tool down to the earth and imagine, visualize, or see earth energy flowing up and into your tool. Turn to the north and direct that energy out, extending it to the edge of your ritual space.

Draw an invoking pentacle in the air, setting a seal or protective barrier in that corner. Allow that earth energy to continue moving through your tool while you turn to the east. Face the east and draw an invoking pentacle in the air, setting a seal or protective barrier. Repeat this process again in the south and the west. Finally, return to the north, where you began, and draw another invoking pentacle to finish the circle.

Move back to the center of your space and draw an invoking pentacle above you, and repeat this process below you.

Your circle is cast. You are between the worlds, and what happens between the worlds changes all the world. So mote it be!

Step Four: Invites

Deciding what allies to invite to your ritual is an important part of the process, and it's often taken for granted. In many circles the entities we invite in, or call, are done almost by assumption. It can feel like just going through the motions when we call huge forces into our circles. Inviting spiritual beings to our rituals is a pretty big deal if you think about it; it should be taken seriously. It's important to ask yourself what best serves the power of the ritual instead of making assumptions based on how "it is always done."

Typically, the elements are called first, followed by deities, ancestors, the Fae, descendants, and more, depending on who you want to invite. It is these "others" that are considered special guests to the ritual. You would call them in if you wanted their energy, influence, or attention on the magick you are performing.

I've discovered over the years that different traditions use different words to describe the invitation process. And, confusingly, some groups used these terms interchangeably, as if they mean the same thing. These words are *invocation* and *evocation*. The two words do have a lot in common, so it's no wonder that different groups use them to refer to the same things. Here's the actual meaning of these words:

- **Invocation:** The process of summoning or calling upon a deity or spirit for their help, assistance, or inspiration.
- **Evocation:** The process of bringing something into the conscious mind.

As you can see, there is a bit of overlap in the meaning of these words. Most common, from what I've found, is using the term *invocation* as a description of inviting spiritual entities and allies into your ritual space.

However, there are groups that use the phrase "invoke the spirit" as a way of describing spirit possession, when a Priestex allows a deity to enter their body.

THE ELEMENTS

In many modern Witchcraft systems, calling in, invoking, or evoking the elements is a pretty common step in the ritual process. It usually happens right after the circle has been cast. Depending on the practice, there are either four or five elements that are called on in ritual space.

Many of the occult groups from the late 1800s used the four classic elements during their rituals. Folks believe the origin of the classic elements comes from ancient Greece.[30] As I've mentioned before, one of the biggest influences on Wiccan and modern Witchcraft rituals was the Order of the Golden Dawn. In Golden Dawn rituals, each of the four elements has a compass point that it is connected to, and within that point there is a watchtower. A magickal being, elemental, or angel serves as the guardian of each of the watchtowers. When the elements are called upon, the guardians of the watchtowers are honored and asked for aid. Most often, this aid comes in the form of their witnessing.

---

30   McMahon, "What Are the Greek Classical Elements?"

The guardians of the watchtowers started out as angels in earlier magickal writings, and they shifted to elemental beings at some point over the years. However, there are practitioners that still work with the watchtowers with angels; others work with elementals.

The Golden Dawn only called upon four elements, as seen in the majority of Wiccan traditions. In other systems of Witchcraft, there are five elements. And there are traditions beyond that that only work with three.

The only thing consistent about Witchcraft is that nothing is consistent.

So now the question is, do we need to worry about the watchtowers, elementals, or even the elements? My answer is pretty heretical: no, we don't.

The concepts of elementals, angels, and watchtowers are from a specific tradition. There is power to these concepts, but this process isn't what makes Witchcraft Witchcraft. This is a specific form for creating ceremonial space. It is from a specific tradition and lineage. Should we know and understand it as modern Witches? Yes, absolutely. But this process isn't required for rituals or for Witchcraft.

Here are the powers connected with the elements.

Air

This element holds the corner of the Witch's pyramid we call *to know*. Air is the sky, clouds, wind, and breath. It is the dawn, the direction of the east, the first break of morning light, and the spring. Air is connected to music and song, communication, words, and thoughts. It is ruled by elementals known as Sylphs. It is the ruler of the suit of Swords in the tarot and is symbolized by humans and the sign of Aquarius. Birds, especially birds of prey, are connected to the element of air. The colors of air are white, light blue, yellow, and rainbow. Incense, feathers, dandelion puffs, seeds, and symbols of flying creatures are all good things to represent air on your altar.

Fire

This element holds the corner of the Witch's pyramid we call *to will*. The element of fire is an outlier because it doesn't exist on its own. It requires the other elements in order to exist, which is why some traditions don't work with fire as one of the elements. Fire is spark, flame, and movement. It is midday, the direction of the south, the peak of the heat of the day, and the summer. Fire is connected to passion, energy, action, and awareness. It is ruled by the elementals known as Salamanders. It is the ruler of the suit of Wands in the tarot and is symbolized by lions and the sign of Leo. Reptiles, like snakes and lizards, are connected to the element of fire. The colors of fire are red, orange, yellow, and white. Candles, images of flames, charcoal, and matches or lighters are all good things to represent fire on your altar.

Water

This element holds the corner of the Witch's pyramid we call *to dare*. Water is the rain, sea, lakes, ponds, and all bodies of water. It is the dusk, the direction of the west, the twilight, and the autumn. Water is connected to depth, inspiration, intuition, and emotions. It is ruled by elementals known as Undines. It is the ruler of the suit of Cups or Chalices in the tarot and is symbolized by eagles and the sign of Scorpio. Fish, sea creatures, and animals that can go between land and sea are all connected to the element of water. The colors of water are blue, green, purple, and white. Bowls of water, seashells, and smooth rocks are all good things to represent water on your altar.

Earth

This element holds the corner of the Witch's pyramid we call *to keep silent*. Earth is the land, rocks, stones, and bones. It is midnight, the direction of the north, darkness or midnight, and the winter. Earth is connected to grounding, bones, ancestors, stability, and connection. It is ruled by the elementals known as Gnomes. It is the ruler of the suit of Pentacles or Coins in the tarot and is symbolized by bulls and the sign of Taurus. Mammals, fossils, plants, and pretty much all land animals are connected to the element of earth. The colors of earth are black, brown, and green. Stones, gems, plant matter, pentacles, and bones are all good things to represent earth on your altar.

Spirit

This element is created when the four sides of the base of the Witch's pyramid connect and make a point. It is made of all four elements, and it is what makes up all four elements. Spirit, also called aether, is not an element that is worked with or acknowledged in all magickal systems.

Spirit is space, the Milky Way, dark matter, atoms, change, and all the things that make up other things. It is not ruled by an elemental and does not have a suit in the tarot. Mythological creatures tend to be connected with spirit. Its direction is center. The colors of spirit are black and white. Anything could be a representation of spirit on your altar. It is the everything and the nothing, the force that holds everything together, the middle, the cauldron, and the unknowable.

As I said before, in many circles it is taken for granted that the elements and the guardians of the elements will be invited to rituals. I feel this is a big misstep in modern Witchcraft for two reasons.

One, it is the height of human hubris to think that we are "inviting" the elements into our ritual's spaces. In case you haven't noticed, the elements are always with us, literally. We are made of earth, air, fire, and water; they are the makeup of our bodies. The elements also exist as forces on our planet. They don't need one human to give them permission to be in a ceremony.

Rather than invoke an element into our circle, perhaps we are better off acknowledging these forces already exist in our circles? Show some reverence and respect for their power.

Two, there is an assumption that we need to go through the process of "invoking" all the elements. Do you really need the energy of *all* these forces in your ritual? Is there a tighter focus for your ceremony? Perhaps we modern Witches need to take a closer look at the *whys* in our rituals. Perhaps we should look at our intentions and ritual plans to see what elements would best serve our ritual.

Personally, I love the pomp and drama of formally acknowledging all the elements. It feels like good spiritual manners to say a hello to each of them when starting the ritual, and to say goodbye at the end. I include elemental invocations in most of my rites because I like how it feels to do so. But I don't think that all Witches must perform their rituals in this manner. It should be up to each individual practitioner to determine if the elemental invocations make sense for the specific ritual that is being performed.

The elements as a whole represent balance and unity, so there is also something to be said for calling in all four (or five).

ELEMENTAL HOME ADVENTURES

One of the best ways to begin to understand the elements is to develop relationships with them. Work through these pieces one at a time. You might even consider spending a week to a month on just one element. In the past, I spent an entire year exploring my relationship to each of the elements. It was a five-year process, but it taught me a lot about myself and the greater world around me. This process should take some time and exploration.

Air Working

When you explore the element of air, wear clothing that matches the colors of air, like yellow and white. Eat foods that are associated with air, like poultry, light or popped foods, and seeds. Visit places that hold a similar energy to the element of air, like mountains or windy places.

✦ *Exercise* ✦

Sit or lie down in a comfortable place. Breathe deeply and feel the flow of air as it comes in and out of your body. Allow your breath to flow and feel the cycle of air as it moves through your body. Allow your awareness to expand, letting the edges of you get wider and less defined.

When you feel ready, imagine or visualize yourself standing safely on a windswept cliff at dawn. Feel the air as it whips over your skin. Look at the world from this height. Face the east and watch as the sun slowly, slowly, slowly rises over the edge of the world. Let yourself see, feel, and explore the power of air.

> *When you feel ready, allow yourself to leave this place of air. Pull in the edges of yourself. Focus on your breath and feel the edges of your body as they become more firm, real, and solid.*
>
> *Repeat this process on a daily basis while you explore this element.*

Fire Working

When you are exploring the element of fire, wear clothing that matches the color of fire, like red and orange. Eat foods that are associated with fire, like charbroiled foods, food cooked over an open flame, peppers, hot or spicy foods, and red, orange, or yellow foods. Visit places that hold a similar energy to the element of fire, like deserts or hot places.

> ### ✦ *Exercise* ✦
>
> *Sit or lie down in a comfortable place. Breathe deeply and feel the energy of your body. Notice how energy flows through your body on its own, moving up and down and keeping things flowing. Allow your awareness to expand, letting the edges of you get wider and less defined.*
>
> *When you feel ready, imagine or visualize yourself standing on the dunes of a hot sandy desert. Feel the heat as it permeates your body. Look at the world through the haze of dry heat. Face the south and look up at the round, red sun in the middle of the sky. Let yourself see, feel, and explore the power of fire.*
>
> *When you feel ready, allow yourself to leave this place of fire. Pull in the edges of yourself. Focus on your breath and feel the edges of your body as they become more firm, real, and solid.*
>
> *Repeat this process on a daily basis while you explore this element.*

Water Working

When you explore the element of water, wear clothing that matches the colors of water, like blue and purple. Eat foods that are associated with water, like fish, seafood, and seaweed. Visit places that hold a similar energy to the element of water, like oceans, lakes, and rivers.

✦ *Exercise* ✦

Sit or lie down in a comfortable place. Breathe deeply and feel the flow of your blood as it moves through your body. Notice how much water your body holds and how it all flows easily without you having to think of it. Allow your awareness to expand, letting the edges of you get wider and less defined.

When you feel ready, imagine or visualize yourself standing safely near the ocean at dusk. Feel the spray of the ocean as it hits your face. Feel the push and pull of the waves as they move in and out. Face the west and watch as the sun slowly, slowly, slowly sets over the edge of the world. Let yourself see, feel, and explore the power of water.

When you feel ready, allow yourself to leave this place of water. Pull in the edges of yourself. Focus on your breath and feel the edges of your body as they become more firm, real, and solid.

Repeat this process on a daily basis while you explore this element.

Earth Working

When you are exploring the element of earth, wear clothing that matches the colors of earth, like green and brown. Eat foods that are associated with earth, like red meat, leafy greens, and root vegetables. Visit places that hold a similar energy to the element of earth, like forests, tree groves, and unspoiled plains or moors.

✦ *Exercise* ✦

Sit or lie down in a comfortable place. Breathe deeply and feel the weight of your bones in your body. Notice how heavy your body is as it relaxes into its natural state. Allow your awareness to expand, letting the edges of you get wider and less defined.

When you feel ready, imagine or visualize yourself standing safely under a canopy of large trees at midnight. Feel the coolness of the air and smell the scent of the trees as you look at the wonder of this place. Look at the shine of the moon as it breaks through the boughs above you. Face the north and look up at the stars and moon in the night sky. Let yourself see, feel, and explore the power of earth.

When you feel ready, allow yourself to leave this place of earth. Pull in the edges of yourself. Focus on your breath and feel the edges of your body as they become more firm, real, and solid.

Repeat this process on a daily basis while you explore this element.

Spirit Working

When you explore the element of spirit, wear clothing that matches the colors of spirit, like black and white. All places are places of spirit, but consider sitting in a darkened room.

✦ Exercise ✦

Sit or lie down in a comfortable place. Breathe deeply and feel the flow of your body doing what it does without you having to think about it or direct it. Allow your breath to flow and feel the cycle of you. Allow your awareness to expand, letting the edges of you get wider and less defined.

When you feel ready, imagine or visualize yourself standing on the edge of the Milky Way. See the vast reaches of space and the swirl of the stars around you. Notice your place in the majesty of it all. Look back at the planet Earth from this vantage point. Let yourself see, feel, and explore the power of spirit.

When you feel ready, allow yourself to leave this place of spirit. Pull in the edges of yourself. Focus on your breath and feel the edges of your body as they become more firm, real, and solid.

Repeat this process on a daily basis while you explore this element.

THE OTHERS

After the elements are honored, acknowledged, or called into your circle, the next step is to do the same for any other spiritual allies you might want as part of your ritual. Choosing what spiritual allies to call into your ritual is an important part of the planning process. Any deities or allies should serve a purpose once invited; it's pretty rude to invite a Goddess to your ritual and then ignore her throughout the whole thing. Make sure any allies called into the ritual are honored and their time is respected.

Deities

There are many reasons to call in deities. You might work with or be dedicated to specific deities and want to ask for their aid or assistance in your ritual. You might call upon Godds that have an energetic signature that matches the type of ritual you are working. As an example, if you are doing a ritual to cast a spell for money, you might call upon the Goddess Fortuna to aid in your work.

There are some lineages of Witchcraft and Wicca that only perform ritual to commune with deities. They go through the process of casting the circle and calling in the elements and then invoke the Godds. Once deities are present, they offer devotion and ask for the deities' blessing on the group's food and drink.

This is all well and good and a perfectly acceptable way to connect with the Godds of Witchcraft and Wicca. However, to me, this ritual format is purely a rite for devotion with no other point. Witchcraft is so much more than devotional ritual. That form of ritual is just one way to practice Witchcraft, not the only way.

There are also thousands of deities to choose from. I don't recommend invoking a deity that you've never heard of just because they might fit the ritual energetic according to your Google search. If you don't currently have a relationship with any deities, at the very least, begin to learn about them, read about them, and explore their power before calling them into a ceremony.

Ancestors

The ancestors are often acknowledged in rituals at specific times of the year, but if you are doing any family rituals, you might also consider calling in ancestors. These could be ancestors of your bloodline, ancestors of the Craft, beloved dead that have passed on during your lifetime, or even the forgotten dead.

Each variation of ancestors will bring a slightly different energy to your rituals. Make sure that your choices for invoking make sense for the ceremony you want to create.

Fae

Inviting in Fae beings, spirits of the land, or other nature spirits is beneficial when doing rituals for earth health, spiritual healing, and connection with the land around you. The "good neighbors," as they are often called, should be considered in the same manner that you might call upon deities. Remember, if you don't have a relationship with them before the ritual, it is a good idea to take some time to develop a relationship with them.

Other Allies

There may be other allies that are unique or specific to you, your group, or your lineage. Other allies could be beloved animal spirits, greenbloods or plant spirits, the descendants, or anything else that feels important for the power of the ritual being created.

In many Reclaiming tradition circles, Time is also invoked as an ally to help all participants stay in the present moment, to do magick in a way that is out of time and space, and to make sure we have enough time to do the work that needs to be done.

Once all of the allies have been invited and welcomed to the ritual, it's time to perform the actual action of the ritual. We will talk more about that on the next page.

Step Five: Action

After you've gone through the process of setting up your "sacred space," it's time to perform the actual rite. In the Reclaiming tradition of Witchcraft, we often refer to this as the *meat* or *tofu* of the ritual. For our purposes, we will refer to this as the action of the ritual.

What is the working you are doing? It is during the action of the ritual that you craft your spell, perform a meditation, do a reading or oracle working, or dozens of other potential options.

It's also important to take into consideration the size of the ritual being performed at this stage. Some types of workings need different attention when being done by a solitary, coven, or large group.

- **Solitary:** Simply a ritual for one. This type of ritual is performed on your own and by yourself. There is a lot of freedom performing solitary rituals, and the only participant you need to worry about is yourself.
- **Coven/Small Group:** Covens and small groups require a bit more forethought and planning. Consider the needs of a small group, which may include waiting while other participants go through a task, moving around a small space, and making sure there are enough supplies for all involved.
- **Large Group:** Large groups require even more detailed planning and, often, more folks to help facilitate the process. The more people attending a ritual, the more needs the participants may have. Consider things like sound, space, comfort, and activities that don't require a lot of waiting.

One of my teachers, Copper Persephone, shared a list with me that was compiled at Reclaiming Samhain Camp in 2004 of all of the potential things you could do for the body of a ritual. The following list is inspired and influenced by what she shared. I have made changes, adjustments, and additions.

This list offers suggestions of the actions or ritual modalities you might choose to perform. It is up to you to determine what actions would best serve the ritual intention you have written. And of course, this is just a jumping-off point; there are plenty of other potential activities not listed here that you might want to do for a ceremony.

ALLY CIRCLE

Best for small group rituals, up to two dozen people (maybe a few more with a strong facilitator or Priestex to lead the process).

During an ally circle, participants literally stand in a circle and take turns stepping into the center of the space to share a truth about themselves. Anyone else in the circle that also holds the statement as their truth steps forward to join the first person. Those in the center acknowledge each other as allies that have something in common. Those still on the edge of the circle honor those that have spoken and shared their truth. The people in the center step back into the circle ring, and the process repeats.

An ally circle works best when there is an overarching theme to the process. I've seen this ritual technology used successfully in rituals for opening a sexual healing temple. Since the theme was sexual healing, the truths that people shared had to do with their own sexual lives, healing, and liberation.

This type of working will typically come to a natural conclusion when the participants have spoken what needs to be said and things start to wind down. It is best to end the working with an acknowledgment of the whole group, the bravery that was expressed, and the witnessing that bonds a group together.

ASPECTING/DEITY WORK/DRAWING DOWN THE MOON OR SUN

Best for small group rituals or large group rituals, but also possible with two people. It is not a practice I would recommend doing as a solitary.

Aspecting is also referred to as "drawing down"; it is the process of allowing deity to utilize a human body. This is an advanced magickal practice and is best performed when the human offering their body has a close relationship with the deity being "drawn down." It is ideal to have another practitioner serve as tender or caretaker of the aspecting Priestex to make sure they are physically safe and comfortable, and also to take notes of anything the deity says during the ceremony.

It works well for the deity to have something to do in the rite once they have been drawn down. Having a Priestex take a deity into their body and then leaving them or ignoring them for the ritual is bad manners and tends to irritate any Godd that has been called in.

In some traditions, "drawing down the moon" is the phrase for aspecting a Goddess or *the* Goddess, and drawing down the sun is the phrase for aspecting a God or *the* God.

DEVOTION
Good for any size group, including solitary.

A devotional ritual can look many different ways in actual enactment, but the energy of the ritual is to show devotion to a spirit or deity. This might happen by giving physical offerings, singing, sharing food or drink, playing music, creating a shrine, telling stories, performing a sacred drama, or something else.

It's good to plan out the devotional pieces of the ritual while keeping in mind the deity you will be working with; different deities appreciate different kinds of offerings.

DIVINATION
Good for any size group, including solitary.

A divinatory ritual is typically used for performing divination for a large issue, problem, or general future visioning. Any form of divination can be used during a divination ritual, including runes, tarot cards, oracle cards, pendulums, bibliomancy, bone reading, ogham, cowrie shells, playing cards, wax reading, scrying, and more.

In a ceremony the divination can be done by a Priestex, by individuals, or in small groups. After the divination has been completed, there can also be a group sharing process on what wisdom came through during the rit-ual as a way to share information and integrate what has been learned.

FOOD
Good for any size group, including solitary.

Cooking, eating, and sharing food is a ritual act any day of the week. But you can also set up ritual space to cook, eat, and share food with intention.

Having a food-focused rite should start during the cooking process or even when the grocery shopping happens. The setting of the table can also be incorporated into the ritual. For more on the practice of food magick, check out the book *The Magick of Food* by Gwion Raven.

INITIATORY/OATH-TAKING
Best for small groups and solitary rituals.

An initiation, elevation, or oath-taking spiritual event is best done in a ritual space. In fact, many traditions require sacred space to be created in a specific way in order for an initiation or elevation to be considered legitimate.

It's pretty common to invite specific deities into initiations, elevations, and oath rituals. Typically, the deities are invited in to witness that rite and acknowledge the new Witch or elevated Witch. Any oaths made in this type of ceremony are often made to a specific deity so the practitioner is held accountable.

LABYRINTH
Good for any size group, including solitary.

A labyrinth ritual is the process of literally walking a labyrinth. There are many different styles and types of labyrinths. However, a labyrinth is not a maze, so this isn't a ritual that you can do at your local pumpkin patch's corn maze in October. A labyrinth has just one path that leads into the center and out again.

One format of labyrinth work is done for meditation and internal reflec-tion. During the walk to the center, or heart, of the labyrinth, you focus on your goal, issue, or problem. Once in the center, you wait for a message or insight to come. When your message has been received, you walk out of the labyrinth and process the message as you leave.

In another format of labyrinth work, you walk to the center of the labyrinth and then cleanse yourself of negative energy or spirits. You then hop out of the labyrinth, leaving the negative spirits to be neutralized in the center.

ORACLE WORK

Good for any size group, including solitary.

Oracle work can be done in tandem with an aspecting ritual or a divination ritual. This type of working is used to gain answers, solutions, or information on the best course of action or the road ahead directly from a deity.

Typically, one Priestex serves as the oracle for the ritual. However, if the oracle rite is being done for a large ritual of thirty or more people, it is good to have several Priestexes serving as oracle throughout the space so ritual participants don't get bored waiting to connect or hear what the oracle has to share with them.

SACRED DRAMA

Best for large groups.

In this type of ritual working, the Priestexes or ritual facilitators reenact a sacred drama or myth. The purpose is twofold: One, the ritual facilitators gain a deeper connection and understanding of the myth or story from a spiritual perspective, specifically from the individual deity's points of view. Two, it allows those watching the sacred drama to see a myth in real time, which also allows for a deeper spiritual understanding of the myth and the deities involved.

SPELLWORK

Good for any size group, including solitary.

There are really only two types of spellwork: calling something toward you and sending something away from you. Spells can take the form of baths, aspurging, smoking, anointing and burning candles, hexing, making mojos or charms, charging objects, releasing and burning, and so much more.

The specific type of spell you desire to cast will help narrow down the type of spell to perform.

SPONTANEOUS

Good for any size group, including solitary.

In a spontaneous ritual, there is no specific plan. The participants follow the flow of energy and see where it leads. The opportunities are endless. This is a big-risk, big-reward type of ceremony. The spontaneity could lead to an amazing, beautiful ritual experience—or it could completely flop and end with ritual participants just awkwardly standing around staring at each other in a circle.

STATIONS

Best for small, medium, or large group rituals.

In this type of rite, stations are set up in the ritual space that participants can interact with. These may be places to write blessings, perform cleansings, do releasing work, create crafts for celebration, place offerings for deities or ancestors, create spells, mourn, laugh, do exercises, plant seeds, hear stories, and so much more.

The stations need to be set up before the ritual begins, much like any altars you want to create, and they should make sense for the type of ritual you are performing. For example, you don't need a ritual station for calling in love when you are performing a ritual for cleansing and protection.

STORYTELLING

Best for medium-to-large group rituals.

Much like sacred drama rituals, storytelling in ritual helps bring a story into a spiritual setting and mindset. The story can be based on a myth or any other story you want to unpack from a spiritual perspective.

Storytelling is best done with a flair for the dramatic and with an invitation for participants to be in a state of active listening. Think about the stories you were told as a child. No doubt the moments of storytelling that you best remember are the ones where the storyteller used voices, facial expressions, and a bit of drama to get you engaged with the story. The same concepts are true when it comes to storytelling in ritual.

TRANCE

Good for any size group, including solitary with modifications.

Going on a trance, journey, or guided meditation during a ritual is probably the most common ritual body format. It's pretty typical to create sacred space, go on a guided journey, and then come back to process the information received. Even though this practice is common, leading a trance or guided meditation is an art form.

Meditation, visualization, trance, journeying, and even self-hypnosis are some of the most powerful practices in a Witch's arsenal. Each of these terms means something slightly different and refers to a specific type of practice. However, they also have a lot in common: all of these practices allow a practitioner the ability to shift awareness, delve deep into the subconscious, and learn information that could never have been received in normal waking life.

Guided visualizations are practices that can be performed on one's own using a pre-recorded set of instructions, or with a coven or large group. There is no such thing as "too big a group" for a guided trance journey—I attended a ritual called Spiral Dance in San Francisco where over two thousand people participated in a trance meditation together. No matter how large the group, guided journeys are an individual experience. They help you discover deeper parts of yourself and provide an opportunity to connect with guides, protectors, and ancestors.

Trance is an altered state of consciousness. Getting into a trance state is entering a hypnotic state of being and is rather similar to self-hypnosis. It's not uncommon in rituals for trances to be led by Priestexes or ritual facilitators, but it is also possible to put yourself into a trance state. In fact, we often go into trance states from mundane activities without even realizing it.

Have you ever driven somewhere, but you weren't really able to remember the full journey once you arrived at your destination? This is because the process of driving is so familiar that your mind can go into a hypnotic state, allowing your consciousness to shift. Obviously, your conscious mind stays engaged because you keep driving the car and arrive where you are headed, but there is some part of you that tunes out and "goes" somewhere else.

Intentional trance allows for you to enter this altered state and connect with your younger self, Godd self, other spirits, and more in order to receive messages, gather information, and/or meet allies.

Effective trance uses hypnotic language, which is the use of positive language to distract the conscious mind (or talking self), all the while seeding your subconscious with affirming words.

Leading a trance is a skill that can be improved with practice. One of my teachers in the Reclaiming Tradition, who is also a skilled hypnotherapist, said that when leading a trance, you have to be in three places at the same time: One, you have to monitor the energy of the people you are leading on the trance. Two, you have to focus on your voice and timing. And three, you have to participate in the trance yourself. Being in three places at once takes practice.

Here are some tips for successfully leading a trance.

Voice

Your voice is a big part of the trance experience. Using your normal speaking voice is fine, but when you slightly adjust the speed, timbre, and meter of your voice, you can help shift the participants into an altered state of being more easily.

When leading a trance, you should also use repetition of images, words, and phrases. From a psychological perspective, this technique is using the power of suggestion and will help you connect with the deep subconscious of those being led through the trance.

Structure

The flow of a trance is very similar to the flow of creating a hypnotic state. Although the structure for any trance is pretty much the same, the specifics and imagery that you use will depend on the type of ritual you are performing and the trance experience you would like to create.

There are four basic steps to leading a trance:

1. **Induction.** The induction is the process of bringing participants into the trance state. During the induction, you will use imagery to help the talking self take a backseat and to appeal to the younger self at the same time. The best way to do this is with tedious tasks that appeal to and distract the talking self. This could be a slow body relaxation process, going through a rainbow of colors, counting backward, or visualizing walking down a staircase.

2. **Action.** Just like the action of a ritual, the action of a trance is the work and point of the trance. This might be a journey to visit a spiritual entity or magickal place. You might trance into a story or a dream. You might trance to the past or the future. No matter where the trance leads, this is the point where the work of the trance is completed.

    At some point during the action of the trance, you have to be silent and allow the participants to have their experience. This is the place where being connected to the participants and your own trance process will be the most important. Timing is always an issue that you need to pay attention to. Knowing when to speak, when to stay silent, how much time and space to give, and when it is time to bring them back from their journey are all parts of trance timing.

    The more trance participants, the more individual needs you will be responsible for. Not everyone will have the same needs during their trance. Some folks trance very easily; they will be able to see, feel, and experience the trance quickly. Other folks will need more time and space; they will need a slower trance experience and longer pauses between your words. Finding a healthy balance between the quicker and slower folks is the key to a good trance.

Participants will also have different sensual connections to a trance. Some people "see" in a trance, almost the same as what we expect from entering a dream state. Although this tends to be the majority of people's experience, it is *not* how all people experience trance. People might see, hear, smell, taste, or have general sensations while in a trance state. It is good to use language that relates to all of these forms of the senses when leading a trance.

This can look like asking trance participants what they can smell on the wind. Ask folks if they can hear anything in the distance. Encourage participants to check in with how they are feeling and notice what messages are coming through. Make sure you create an experience that allows for more than just visual processing.

3. **Takeaway.** Once it is time to bring folks back from the trance experience, you want to make space for a takeaway. This could be a gift, symbol, or message that should be brought into their waking life. This is also the moment to share gratitude for the experience in the trance. A thank you and a moment for goodbyes should happen at this time.

4. **Return.** There is a process for entering the hypnotic state, and that process should be reversed to return from that state. The return is a calling back from the places folks have been traveling to. Whatever imagery was used to get people into a trance state, the reverse should be used to get them out. This is another moment for your tone and timbre to shift, from a trance-leading voice into something closer to your normal speaking voice.

Blood

Blood is the force that keeps flow happening in our bodies. The power of blood keeps nutrients moving to our organs. Blood moves in our veins, our hearts, and our brains—it is the delivery service of our bodies. Our blood is also a unique signature; we have different blood types, some more rare than others. It is a life force that literally connects us to our ancestors.

The Blood of Ritual is the water-like influence of the ritual and the intuitive, in-the-moment pieces that are hard to plan. It is the place where we must leave room for mystery. The Blood of Ritual is what brings in our emotional connection; it is what helps us be moved and connect to magick in a way that is beyond our thinking self.

The Blood of Ritual is what makes our rituals alive. It is the sometimes-ineffable thing that comes through and helps us all feel that something magickal is happening. These are the parts of ritual that stick with us and that we remember years down the road.

Creating a ritual is building a story. There is a foundation setting, there is a peak of energy, and then there is the wrap up. The flow of this process, and getting from one step to the next, is the Blood of Ritual. These pieces need to help move us forward in the story, and they need to do so with grace and art.

In this section on the Blood of Ritual, we will go over energy raising and what to do once the activities of the ritual are completed. We will go into the performance part of ritual and how to balance putting on a show with putting on a rite. The section on the Blood of Ritual is the smallest of the three (Breath, Bone, and Blood). This is because the Blood is where the unknown happens. It can only happen when it happens! It is the part of ritual that is incredibly difficult to quantify, explain, or even plan. The Blood of Ritual is where the real magick happens!

After the Body: What Comes Next?

Once the body of the ritual is completed, it might feel like things are complete. You've done the thing that you came to do, but the ritual isn't over—there is still more to do. The energy that has been building from creating sacred space and performing your ceremony now needs to be charged, grounded, or moved.

Traditionally, after the action, there is a process of energy raising. This is really common in public rituals where there may be a group dance or song. This process allows all participants' voices to come together and put energy toward the ritual's goal. More often than not, this is needed for a ritual to have a deep impact.

After the energy is another false ending. When the energy raising is done and settled, there is still more to do: a good wrapping up of the experience. Getting some closure on the work that was done, sometimes called a benediction, will help participants mentally shift from the magick of ritual into preparing to return to "normal life."

Finally, we have to say goodbye to all the forces and entities that we invited into the ritual. The ritual can only be complete when we have said goodbye to the loved ones that came to the party. After the body, there is still magick to do.

Step Six: Raising Energy

Ideally after the body piece of the ritual, you move into raising energy. This energy is raised to "feed" the working you've performed, to activate it, and send your desire/goal out into the world. After the energy raising peaks, there should be a moment of holding to allow the energy to settle or spill out toward your success.

There are many ways to raise energy. Think about if you've ever been to a dance club. At a club, there is loud music throbbing and people are enjoying themselves. It is easy to get swept up into that energy. Think about if you've ever been to a sporting event. You sit in the stands with a crowd of people. You all root together, cheer together, and mourn together. This is the power of group energy. This is one of the things we work to create in rituals.

There may be times when a ritual doesn't need an energy raising, but rather the energy needs to be put to bed or grounded. There are rituals where the energy needs to be dispersed and cleared. It will be up to you to determine what is the most appropriate, and beneficial, way to work with ritual energy.

Here are some of the most common ways to raise energy in a ceremony.

CHANTING

Chanting isn't exactly like singing, although the two things do have commonalities. With chanting, those participating in the ritual will all recite the same words over and over again. Typically, these are rhyming words in short sentences that are easy to remember. Often when chanting in ritual, the participants' voices will get louder and louder until a moment comes where everyone simply just stops. No joke, this happens all the time. There is no logical explanation—it's simply magick.

In some traditions of Witchcraft, the High Priestess will signal when it is time to stop, but in many other traditions you keep chanting until the group stops. Chanting may be used in tandem with several other energy-raising modalities.

DANCING

Physical movement is an excellent way to raise energy; however, this modality isn't always inclusive for all participants—and that needs to be taken into consideration when planning your rituals.

Dancing can be freeform and chaotic, or it can be a specific set of movements. For example, the spiral dance is a very popular dance for energy raising. It is easy to do, with no steps needing to be taught—it's basically just a shuffle to the left. The leader of the spiral dance is really the only person that needs to know how to do it; the rest of the participants follow along. For participants that may have mobility issues, they can sit in the center of the ritual space during a spiral dance and still fully participate in the energy raising.

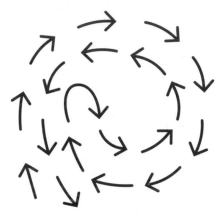

Spiral Dance

Skipping, jumping, or a quick shuffle around your ritual space is also considered dancing. Just like with chanting, dancing is done until the moment where enough energy has been raised. There should be a level of ecstasy that is reached before the movement stops. This modality can also be used in tandem with several other energy-raising options.

DRUMMING

Drums are a powerful energy-raising tool. But there is also something about the rhythmic pulse of drumming that engages all ritual participants. Drumming is best utilized in combination with dancing, singing, or chanting.

Drumming for the purpose of playing music is not the same as drumming for a ritual. I've played drums for large rituals with skilled and professional drummers, but they knew nothing of ritual technology or riding the energy of a ceremony. A skilled musician does not a good ritual drummer make!

Of course, you need some sort of drumming or rhythmic skill to drum in ritual. If you can't maintain a heartbeat drum at a solid and steady rate, practice that first before moving into more complex ritual-drumming patterns.

There is also potential for the drums to take over or "push" the energy of a ritual. This isn't ideal. Drumming should support the ritual participants and help carry the energy raising, but it should not push, force, or attempt to control the energy-raising process.

Music

Music is a great way to raise energy, and it allows for so many options. Music can be played live during rituals with musicians and instruments, and it can also be prerecorded or electronic. You don't have to stick to Pagan, classical, new age, or folk music in your rituals—modern music works too!

Music sets a mood, so it's important to pick music for your ceremonies carefully and with intention. Make sure the music you select matches the energy you want to create. If you are going to use music for energy raising, that music should be upbeat and steady or increasing in speed. Music is typically a vehicle for movement; together, they work really well to raise energy.

Sex Magick

Raising energy with sex can be done solo, with a couple, or with a group. It is important that all participants hold the focus and intention of the ritual and send that intention out at the point of orgasm. Even more important: all participants must consent and know that magick is being worked.

Singing

Much like live music, singing allows for a lot of energy-raising options in ritual. The thing about singing is it brings participants together. All of the ritual participants' voices come together, and that has a way of feeding ritual energy that can't be matched with recorded music. When voices join together, it creates a magick on its own. By singing songs that have words matching the intention of your ritual, you can add another layer of power to your rituals.

TONING

Toning is just singing without words. When you are uncertain how you want to raise energy or when it feels like the ritual needs an energy boost or energetic shift, toning is a great way to create that power.

———◆◆———

PUTTING THE ENERGY TO BED

As I mentioned before, sometimes energy doesn't need to be raised, but needs to be sent into the earth or dispersed. When you perform a ritual where energy doesn't need to be sent anywhere or there isn't anything being charged, take some time to send the energy down into the earth. This can be done by simply placing your hands on the ground and allowing any built-up energy to flow out of you and into the ground. You can also send the energy where it needs to go. I often imagine a mycelial layer of the earth, this mushroom-like network that flows over the planet. By sending any excess or built-up energy into this network, it will go where it is most needed.

Performance: Art and Theatre

Now we come to the parts of ritual that are hard to explain and hard to put into practice. There is a layer of ritual that is performative. There is a layer of ritual that needs to be entertaining and engaging in order to keep all participants fully engaged in the magick. This is tricky.

The performance of ritual is a fine line. If you lean too far toward performance, your ritual will lose its magick. A ritual that is too focused on performance will turn into a beautiful package, a finely wrapped present, with nothing of substance inside. If there's too much focus on creating the perfect performance in your planning, your ritual becomes all sparkle and no substance. And of course, this becomes a larger issue as the ritual participant numbers increase.

Rituals that focus too much on presentation can also create a situation where the participants feel like they are watching other people have a ritual, rather than participating in one themselves. It's fine to go and watch a ritual being performed, but it is so much more impactful to go and partic-ipate in one.

I've attended rituals that were all sparkle and no substance; one in par-ticular really stands out for me. Ahead of time, the ritual was hyped up all over social media. It was being led by some popular, well-known Witches, and expectations were high. I kept hearing "Get there early because we are going to run out of space!" For months the facilitators had been posting tidbits about what participants could expect. And I was excited!

Arriving at the ritual, the room was beautifully decorated. The lights were dim, with candles and twinkly lights all around the space. Music was playing, creating an air of mystery and magick.

After all of the participants arrived, the ritual Priestexes, who were dressed in fancy regalia, spoke to us in dramatic, theatre-style voices of the myster-ies that would be revealed to us and of the deep magicks we would explore. When the invocations began, they were beautifully performed. The Priestexes were all well-spoken; it was clear that the ritual had been rigorously rehearsed. There was something slightly inorganic about the ritual, but that wasn't the problem.

Once the invocations were complete, at the moment when the action of the ritual should have begun, we were told to stand and open our arms and receive the power of the open portal. We did, and then … That was it. The devocations began, the closing of sacred space started, and just like that, the ritual was over. I remember thinking, *That's it?* What a disappointment!

The ritual was all sparkle and no substance. The desire to create some-thing beautiful, dramatic, and aesthetically Witchy overrode the fact that it was supposed to be a rite with a magickal purpose.

The other side of the coin is that a ritual with no flair or performance can feel rote, boring, and uninspired. Witches need inspiration in their rit-uals. Without a bit of drama, a ritual can quickly begin to feel like watch-ing someone read from a dictionary. Informative, maybe even interesting, but not engaging or fun.

I've also attended rituals where there was no drama, no flair, and no rit-ual performance even taken into consideration. The Priestexes read a ritual from a three-ring binder, almost like they were reading out loud in ninth-grade English class. And although the magickal intent was met, the ritual was boring and dry. The magick fell flat because there was no performance piece to hold it up. There was nothing to experience.

Again, this is a delicate balance.

The other complication with performance is that it's an additional skill that isn't necessarily connected to Witchcraft or spirituality. Not all Witches are going to be natural performers, and some may have no interest in performance arts in any way. For some Witches, even the idea of performance will be a turnoff.

I've heard very serious practitioners say that performance is fluff and unnecessary to true magick. I call BS. Performance is what calls and awakens our emotional self, which needs to be engaged in ritual in order for there to be any impact whatsoever.

Much of these concepts won't matter if you are performing a ritual as a solitary; you don't need to worry about ritual participants' experience when you are the only participant. However, the more people that get involved, the more awareness you will want to have with these key pieces of ceremony.

RITUAL COSTUMING

What you wear during a ritual will impact your ritual experience and the experience of the participants. Imagine going to a devotional ritual for Aphrodite and the Priestex of the ritual has dirt on their face, dirty hair, cargo shorts, and a stained T-shirt. I mean, you can show up for the Godds however you'd like, but for an Aphrodite ritual, I would imagine the ritual facilitators would be adorned in something luscious and beautiful.

For the people Priestexing the ritual, your garb will help you stand out as a leader. Ritual garb can help you to shift into a more magickal mindset. Make sure that ritual costumes fit correctly, are easy to move in, and are not totally uncomfortable to wear. Trying on your costuming ahead of time will help you be sure that the clothes work for you and not against you.

For coven and solitary work, having dedicated ritual robes or other forms of adornment will make it easier for you to shift into a magickal state of mind. Taking off your mundane clothes and stepping into your ritual garb is a touchstone to remind yourself that you are going to do magick now. Sliding on a ritual bracelet or tying ritual cords around your waist helps you shift into that place as well.

RITUAL MAKEUP

Makeup isn't modern; it's ancient—there is evidence of makeup being used in ancient Egypt as a form of ritual adornment. Makeup can do a lot for a ritual performance. Look at the power of drag makeup as an example of what kind of transformations makeup can create.

Makeup can help you shift into the energy of a deity or spiritual ally. Makeup can help you to step deeper into mystery. Makeup has the potential to shift your energy and focus. This shift will have an impact on those serving as Priestex, and also on those seeing the made-up ritualists.

One of the most powerful ritual makeup experiences I had was when another participant did their makeup ahead of time as an homage to the magick of the ritual they were attending. They were not one of the Priestexes, but they were inspired by the ritual intention. They painted their skin gold and wore a shimmering dress. Their look was inspiring and helped me, as another ritual participant, sink deeper into mystery. It helped me remember that we were in altered space during our rite and that anything was possible.

RITUAL LIGHTING

Lighting is really a big deal. If your room is too bright, the ritual might feel sterile. I've attended rituals in rooms with fluorescent lights. Although the ritual was lovely, the lighting was annoying and distracting. It would have been better if the overhead lights were off and a few floor lamps or strands of twinkly lights were used instead.

If your room is too dark, people won't be able to see what is going on. I once helped lead a ritual where we had turned the lights down to create the right atmosphere, but the space we were using for the ritual didn't have a lot of options for muted lighting. With the main lights off, it was too dark for some of the participants. During the beginning of the ritual, one of the participants jumped up, interrupting the Priestex in the middle of their invocation, to complain about how dark it was and how she wanted to be able to see other participants' faces.

You might also want to consider what one of my teachers calls "the holy sacred lighting change." Perhaps you want to keep the lights brighter until a trance begins, then turn the lights down, only to bring them up a tiny bit for the energy raising. Playing with lighting will help shift the mood of the participants.

RITUAL AESTHETIC

What is the overall vibe of your rite and how can you create this as part of your ritual's aesthetic? The aesthetic can be played out in the following ways:

+ **Altars:** Who or what will you create altars for, and how will you decorate them?
+ **Backstage:** Is there a place in your location where the ritual Priestexes can sequester themselves to allow for pre-ritual preparation? This would also be a place where you can store other items, like storage bins and boxes, that don't need to be in the ceremony space.
+ **Decor:** Do you need to bring in lighting, wall coverings, ritual supplies, or other supplies to help you create the right visuals in your space?
+ **Entry:** Will you need to set something in the entryway to welcome people into the space and help them to enter into the ritual in the right spiritual frame of mind?
+ **Staging:** Do you need to set up an area for specific ritual participants or Priestexes? For example, do you need an area specifically blocked off for musicians or drummers? Will you need a kids' area or a place for folks with mobility needs? Will participants be arranged in rows with Priestexes in the "front" of the room, or in a circle with the Priestexes in the middle?

RITUAL VOICE

There are ways to adjust the tone and timbre of your voice to help impact the energy of the ritual. But before we get into that, there are some basic voice concepts you need to understand.

If you are speaking to a large group, you need to make sure that everyone can hear you. One of the tricks they teach in theatre training is to speak to the back of the room. Your voice needs to carry in a way that even someone at the very back of the space can hear you without it seeming like you are yelling at folks. If you have trouble projecting your voice, you can practice this or even get voice lessons and training.

Each ritual location will impact your voice in different ways. Outdoor venues will swallow up more of your voice than indoor locations. The bigger the place, the more you will need to project. And there are lots of weird little structural things at different locations that could impact the volume of your voice. It's good to test for these things before ritual participants arrive.

One of the places I taught a lot of classes was a yurt on my teacher's property. A yurt is a round transportable space with a cone-shaped roof. When we would stand in the center of the yurt our voices would echo, but only to those folks also standing in the center of the yurt. To the rest of the room, our voices would sound totally normal. If you weren't prepared for that little anomaly, it had the potential to totally throw you off what you were saying.

You may want to use different voices for invocations, leading trances, performing sacred dramas, or storytelling. Here are some different "voices."

- **Loud:** Using this vocal method, you can shout, scream, or yell to impose the importance of your words. This may be done for a storytelling effect, to shake people up, to get attention, or to simply make sure you are heard. Just to be clear, speaking loudly is very different from yelling. There are degrees of loudness; choose wisely.
- **Silent:** Saying nothing at all actually speaks volumes. Using silence as a means of getting attention, expressing emotion with your body, or shaking up the energy of the room can be really powerful.

- **Soft:** A soft voice needs to be used when you already have people's attention. If you try to use a soft voice when all of the ritual participants are talking to each other, no one will hear you. A soft voice encourages people to lean in closer and focus on your words. Soft voice can convey tenderness, sweetness, or deep emotion.
- **Trance:** A trance voice is slow, measured, and methodical. It is best used when leading a trance, but it can also be used in storytelling or for invocations.
- **Whisper:** Much like a soft voice, a whisper encourages participants to lean in and listen closely. A whisper also conveys a sense of secrecy. It makes people feel like you are going to reveal something they don't want to miss.

When doing an invocation, you also want to use language that is evocative and powerful. If doing an invocation for Aphrodite, you wouldn't just say:

> *We call you, Aphrodite. Hail and welcome.*

The words are correct, but the meaning is weak—that just doesn't do it. However, you might say something like:

> *Beautiful Goddess Aphrodite, daughter of the foaming sea, lover of all sensual delights, we call to you to join our circle. Blessed one of love and passion, be here now to lend your wisdom and delight us with your beauty. Hail and welcome Aphrodite!*

Speaking like this not only appeals to the entity you are invoking, but it also appeals to the ritual participants.

Ritual Music

Just like the score of a movie, the music of a ritual can really impact emotion and how things are received by participants. Music should support the ritual and add to the experience. It's important to keep the reins on music so it doesn't end up being a musical show, but a support piece of the rite.

Music and drumming can help set the tone for a trance, storytelling, and energy raising. However, music isn't something that you can just insert into a ritual when you don't have any musical experience. If you've never played an instrument before, picking it up for ritual isn't the best thing to do.

Playing music for a ritual is also different than playing music for a performance. Ritual musicians have to be able to pay attention to the energy. It will need to be watched and measured while playing music. You need to be engaged with the participants, unlike a performance, where the participants need to be engaged with the performers. The music may need to raise, lower, or stop completely depending on what is going on with the Priestex and the participants.

RITUAL TRANSITIONS

One of the more challenging parts of a ritual are the moments that move participants from one step to the next. There is an art and a flow to transitions. These moments should be graceful, as if you are seamlessly moving from one step to the next. This might sound easy, but it's not.

Let's say you are in the process of leading a trance and then want the participants to start a spiral dance. You have to get folks from a relaxed state, where they may be lying down, into an ecstatic state, where they need to be standing up and moving.

If folks are lying, down you can't just clap your hands and shout, "Okay people, everyone stand up! It's dancing time!" Although this might be an effective way to get people into the next piece of the ritual, it is clunky and inelegant. For participants, this type of transition can feel jarring, and it can pull people out of the magick.

It's better to say something like, "As you begin to integrate the messages from your journey, allow your body to start to move. Let yourself stand and connect in with the power of the land and the Witches around you. Let's join together in a circle." This would be an ideal moment to start a song or chant to help further bring people into the next part of the ritual.

The Final Step: Closing the Ritual

Once you've done the body of the ritual and raised energy to charge your working, you might think, *Okay,* now *the ritual is over,* but it's not. There is still more work to do. Now it's time to say thank you and goodbye to any allies you invited to the ceremony and release the circle that you've built. Honestly, this is a process of respect and good spiritual hygiene.

When you call in spiritual energy and build up ritual containers, you need to do something to disperse that. This is good for keeping your spiritual energy clear, but more important is the acknowledgment of the allies that you've called in. Think about being invited to a party and then kicked out without being thanked for coming or wishing you a fond farewell. It's just rude.

Deciding when this moment happens can be a challenge. This is another one of those transitional moments. You have to pay attention to the energy and feel when it is time to move on.

In the Reclaiming tradition, after the energy raising, we will often have a benediction. This is a moment when a Priestex wraps it all up. They take a moment to talk about what we have done and the magick of the moment. It gives the participants a chance for closure before saying goodbye to the spiritual allies that have been called in.

Not all traditions have a benediction moment; they just move forward and perform the next step of the ritual. There isn't a right or a wrong way to do this. But as a participant, I find the benediction helpful for my experience of the ritual.

DEVOKING

The process of releasing the energies and entities that were invited in is called *devoking.* Yep, just the opposite of invoking. Most often, allies and elements are released in the opposite order of how they were called in. Thank that entity/energy that you called in, express your gratitude, and send them on their way. The phrase "Hail and Farewell" is often used to end a devocation and fully dismiss that entity.

In some traditions, people feel that the devoking should be a quick process, a simple releasing of the energies that have been built up. There is some truth to this. Yes, you should be able to release the energies more quickly than it took to build them up, but it is also important that this releasing take the time it needs. In the devoking process, we are saying goodbye and expressing our gratitude to powerful spiritual forces—it's just plain rude to be like, "Okay, thanks, peace out."

The paradox of taking your time is that you have to remember that ritual participants might be totally wiped out by this point. If you take a really long time using all sorts of flowery language to devoke the elements and the Godds, you might lose your audience. In a devocation, you want to have brevity with impact.

Whatever entity was called into your ritual last is who you will say goodbye to first. Address them with gratitude. Speak out loud how their energy and influence helped build your ritual. Thank them for spending the time with you. And when you have said what needs to be said, end that with "Hail and farewell." Go through all "the others," then all of the elements that you spoke to during the invocations.

RELEASING

Once the allies and elements have been sent back to their lovely realms, the next step of the releasing process is to open the circle. Sometimes this is called closing the circle, releasing the circle, or taking down the circle. The words might be different, but they all mean the same thing: you are releasing the energy that you built up at the beginning.

Of course, there are also some traditions of Witchcraft where the circle is not opened or released, but rather left to dissipate on its own. I think this is a fine option if no one will randomly walk through your ritual space unknowingly. Again, it's a matter of spiritual hygiene. You wouldn't leave your used wet towel in the middle of the hallway for someone else to deal with. (Right?!) It's the same with your circle.

To release the circle, use the same magickal tool that you used to create the circle. You might cut open the circle, call that energy back into your tool, or break open any energy that has built up. If you used invoking pentacles to create your sacred space, you would then want to use banishing pentacles to clear out those locks and borders you made for your circle.

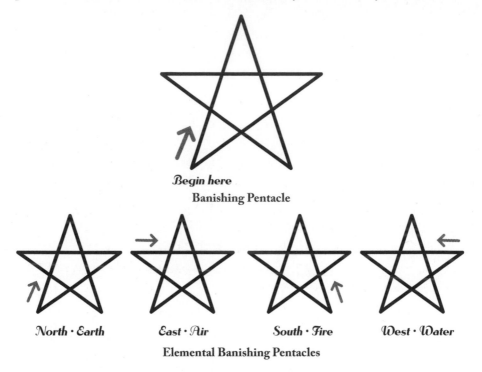

Begin here
Banishing Pentacle

North · Earth   *East · Air*   *South · Fire*   *West · Water*
Elemental Banishing Pentacles

PROCESSING

Once the circle is open, the ritual is done! Yay! Congrats! However, there is another step of ritual that is often overlooked, forgotten, or not openly spoken about in magickal circles. A ritual can shake things up in your life, create an emotional reaction, or open up unprocessed stuff for you. After a rite, it's a good idea to write down your feelings and experience. You might not have the capacity to deal with any issues that come up right away, but you don't want to lose the post-ceremony feelings or any insights that came to you. Writing it down will give you the information to process later.

Depending on the type of ritual, you might also need to ground and center again, drink some water, or eat something to help you come fully back to your body. You might want to drink something with sugar in it, eat a bit of chocolate, or put a pinch of salt under your tongue to help you prevent a ritual hangover the next day.

CAKES AND ALE OR WINE

This part of a ritual is sometimes called "cakes and ale" and sometimes "cakes and wine." The phrase "cakes and ale" actually originated with the play *Twelfth Night* by Shakespeare.[31] It is used to refer to a time when there were no worries. The first time the phrase "cakes and wine" was used in reference to Witchcraft was in Gerald Gardner's book *Witchcraft Today*. In his later writing, *The Meaning of Witchcraft*, he referred to this piece of the ritual as "cakes and ale."[32] So, we could argue that the concept of ritual celebration featuring cakes and ale came from Shakespeare, to Gardner, to us modern Witchcraft practitioners.

The ritual moment of cakes and ale (or wine) should have a little asterisk next to it, because it is one of the parts of ritual that seems to go in many different directions—or not at all, depending on the specific tradition or practice.

In some traditions, cakes and ale is an integral part of the ritual, one that is done in the middle of things as a blessing to the participants. After the deities are "drawn down," those deities bless the food and drink and then the ritual participants consume the food and drink, literally taking in the energy of the Godds. This has always felt a bit like the taking of communion in a Christian church to me. In many of these traditions, this is performed as a sacred rite called the Great Rite, which is a union of the polarities of masculine and feminine.

In other traditions, the cakes and ale is done after the ritual working and raising energy is completed. It is done at this point to help participants ground after expending the energy it takes to raise magickal power. It is a way to reconnect with the mundane world and remember that our bodies need fuel.

---

31   The Free Dictionary, s.v. "cakes and ale," accessed July 26, 2022, https://idioms.thefreedictionary.com/cakes+and+ale.

32   Mankey, "All About Cakes and Ale."

Some traditions leave the cakes and ale until the ritual is totally complete and done and the circle is opened. Typically, when cakes and ale land in this part of the process, it becomes more of a social time for ritual participants to hang out, but it also serves to help participants ground. Socialization might sound silly or frivolous, but it is an important part of a coven or group coming together and bonding with each other.

And, of course, there are also folks who don't do any form of cakes and ale at all.

Pitfalls and Problems

Even with the most detailed and careful planning, mistakes will still happen. It's all part of the magick. Mistakes are an important part of learning how to be in the flow of a ritual. It's easy to step into full-on bridezilla mode when something goes sideways in your carefully constructed ritual plan. However, the rituals with errors and mistakes are the ones we tend to learn the most from as ritual facilitators.

Errors are the moments when we can really step into the magick and allow mystery to be an ally. The more you try and control every second of a ritual, the harder it is to go with the flow and let things unfold in a way that serves mystery the best.

MISTAKES

Yep, mistakes are going to happen. You're going to jump the line and start your invocation early. You're going to forget the transition word so the next Priestex isn't aware it's their turn to step in for an invocation. You're going to forget to light the sacred candle or burn the sacred incense.

In a public ritual, you might phrase something clumsily and accidentally offend a participant. You might not speak loud enough and have your piece of the ritual drowned out by the sound of a truck driving by. You might forget the words to the song you're teaching and have to get backup from another Priestex. All of these are things I have done while helping lead a public ritual.

Even when doing rituals on your own, you will make mistakes, forget things, stumble over the words, or accidentally leave things out. It's just that when doing it on your own, there aren't any other witnesses to your blunders.

Just know, right here and now, that mistakes are going to happen—and you won't get in trouble for it. The Witchcraft police aren't going to come by and scourge you when you make a mistake. Your house won't collapse if you say the words of an invocation in the wrong order, and things won't blow up in your face if you forget to light the sacred candle. The universe is a much more forgiving place than you might think.

While we are on the subject of mistakes:

+ Rituals are allowed to be silly, fun, and playful. Even if your ritual is serious and stoic, if you make a mistake and start laughing, that's okay!
+ Sometimes mistakes actually help the ritual turn a corner or play out better than your original plan might have been leading to.
+ Be connected and aware of the energy of the ritual. You might need to course correct or shift your plan mid-ritual depending on the flow of energy. Being too rigid about your plan can be problematic and block the power you're building.
+ Remember all your supplies. Make a list ahead of time of all the props and implements you will need. But also remember the safety measures you might need for these props. For example, if you are going to have a fire in a cauldron, you will need a lid for that cauldron to tamp down the fire, and you will need to be sure the cauldron is sitting on a heatproof surface. Have you ever burnt a tablecloth with the feet of a hot cauldron? I have. Not fun.
+ Remember you are creating a ritual to facilitate an experience for people (including yourself). All you can do is open the door; you can't force or control what actually ends up happening. If you try to force or control an experience, it is bound to fail.

When you are creating a ritual with other people, you also have to deal with other people's mistakes. It's important to keep an attitude of calmness and openness. If someone else makes a mistake and forgets their lines or their cue, you can't let that derail the energy. Keep going and find the best way forward.

Problems

On top of mistakes, your rituals will also run into problems. Preplanning can go a long way in helping to avoid problems. But there will always be circumstances beyond your control or planning. Again, roll with the punches as best you can. You don't have to take any issues personally. From rental hall issues to bad weather to forgetting an important ritual implement, problems in rituals are going to happen.

When you rent a hall for a gathering or larger event, you have a lot more to remember and double-check. I once showed up to a rental hall and the person that was supposed to meet me to open the building didn't show up. No one answered the phone number I had, and they already had my money! When working with a rental facility, have all your contracts signed, and ask for more than one person's contact information in case there are issues!

Rituals outdoors have less problems with it comes to facility issues and people unlocking the doors, but you can have issues with the weather, and even sometimes the wildlife. You can't always plan for weather; hot is hot. But having fans, coverings, and other means of protection from weather should always be a part of your backup plan.

It's also a good idea to alert participants when weather might be an issue. Folks can look up that information on their own, but they might not. If you are expecting rain, let folks know what your plans are to deal with rain. If it's going to be blistering hot, remind folks to bring water, hats, fans, or anything else they might need for their comfort.

There will always be rituals where a Priestex forgets some important tool or feature for the ritual. Gathering at least a couple of hours before the ritual to go over the outline will help you find these missing pieces before the ritual starts. You don't want to be lining people up to dance the Maypole only to realize you've got no ribbons! Do a final check of supplies at least an hour ahead of time so last-minute adjustments can be made.

If tools are missing, you can always use the toolbox of your body as a replacement. Look back at "Tools: Do You Need Them?" for bodily alternatives for potential tools that could be used during rituals.

SAFETY

We Witches work with a lot of fire in our rituals. From cauldrons to candles, we have a lot of open flame going on around us. Fire safety is a thing we all need to remember. And unfortunately, even when we are safe and take all of the precautions, mistakes with fire can happen.

I can't stress fire safety enough. I've seen a lot of fire situations go sideways in rituals. And I know two people who lost their homes due to candles burning out of control. One of these folks lost their lives due to a house fire from candles. Don't assume your fire is safe. Never leave flames unattended. Have things on hand to smother or squash any flames that might get out of control.

There was a ritual where the Priestex leading the activity had a cauldron in the center of the room with a faerie fire burning in it. A faerie fire is made with Epsom salt and rubbing alcohol. It is a low-heat fire, but it's still fire nonetheless. She wanted to make the fire bigger by pouring more rubbing alcohol into the burning cauldron. This is not the correct way to work with faerie fire—faerie fire needs to be smothered. Then the ingredients are increased and the fire is relit. So, when she poured in the rubbing alcohol, the bottle of alcohol caught on fire like a Molotov cocktail. If it wasn't for the quick thinking of one of the other participants, who saw it happen and smothered the fire, the Priestex could have seriously hurt herself.

In my second-degree Gardnerian elevation ritual, I leaned over the altar and caught a huge piece of my hair on fire. At the time, my hair was waist length, and I lost a good five inches from one section of my hair. Inches of my hair were floating around the room. If it wasn't for my HP and HPS, I would have lost a lot more. Never take safety for granted when working with fire in a ritual.

Animals and wildlife can be fun when they show up in ritual, but wild animals are just that—wild. At outdoor gatherings, be aware and cautious of the wildlife around you. I'll never forget the time a skunk joined one of my new moon rituals. Thankfully, that sweet little skunk ran along the edge of the circle we had cast and never came any closer, but there were a few moments when we prepared to run.

Once, while teaching in Australia, I learned very quickly that rituals needed to stay off a particular area of the lawn after several folks had leeches on their legs from being in the grass. Although not life-threatening, leeches are no fun to deal with. The last thing you want during ritual is to lie in the grass for a trance and then find yourself covered in leeches.

Other people can also cause issues during ritual. Typically, the folks you've invited to participate in the ritual aren't the issue, although this can also happen. More likely, outsiders or passersby have the potential to cause problems.

At a large Pagan conference one year, a group of intoxicated men wandered into our hotel. They were Christian and found our convention to be against their Godd. They were looking to cause problems and start a fight. Luckily, the group I was with was calm and patient, and we walked them out of the hotel while alerting security of their presence.

RITUAL HANGOVERS

There are rituals where you have a deep emotional reaction, are spiritually moved, or run a lot of energy through your body. If you don't take care of yourself after the ritual, typically by doing something as simple as drinking water and/or eating something, you might end up feeling a bit magickally hungover the next day.

A ritual hangover feels a lot like an alcohol-induced hangover. It can physically manifest as:

- ◆ Having a headache.
- ◆ Feeling excessively tired.
- ◆ Having excess energy.
- ◆ Feeling dizzy.
- ◆ Being nauseous.

+ Having difficulty letting go of the ritual.
+ Noticing challenging emotions coming up.
+ Feeling disconnected from your body.
+ Being cranky.

At the very least, have a nice glass of water after any ritual to help clear your physical body and to help prevent a yucky feeling the next day.

GAINING EXPERIENCE

An important, and yet difficult piece, of the Blood of Ritual is the fact that the more you practice, the more you try, and the more experience you gain, the better your rituals will become. But we live in a culture where we want immediate gratification. We want to just have the credentials to do the thing. You can sign up for Witchcraft classes online, read, chat, and gain understanding of ritual concepts, but this isn't experience.

Experience takes time. It is a slow process that can feel hard when you're in the middle of it. Gaining experience means making mistakes, having slipups, and trying new things. Time, testing, and experimentation are your friends when it comes to gaining experience.

As you deepen your ritual skills (and your Witchcraft in general), let things unfold slowly. Don't be in a rush to be perfect. The journey is the destination. Your ritual skills will never stop evolving, and you will never stop learning how to create better rituals. Enjoy the process and let it unfold. It isn't a race.

Creating Your Own Rituals

We modern Witches and Pagans have had many rituals and celebrations handed down to us. Many of us may have been told, or may believe, that these rituals and celebrations are eons old and were practiced by pre-Christian peoples. Unfortunately, that's not the truth—at least not completely. The celebrations and rituals that have been handed down to us in the modern age are beautiful, wonderful, and totally work; however, many of them, if not most, came into being in the mid-twentieth century.

This can be a hard truth to swallow if you've gone your entire practice believing esbat full moon rituals are thousands of years old, handed down by groups of hidden people keeping Witchcraft alive. I know it was a hard pill for me to swallow. But knowing that a specific ritual practice isn't ancient doesn't mean it isn't powerful or doesn't work. And truth speaks to power.

The rituals you already know or might read about in other books published from the 1950s to the early 2000s are modern. They aren't modern versions of older rituals; they are modern rituals. Many were *inspired* by the occult writings of the 1500s all the way through to the 1800s, but many of the folks writing those rituals didn't consider what they were doing Witchcraft. They referred to themselves as occultists, alchemists, and spiritualists, but not Witches.

For the most part, our modern Witchcraft rituals are just that: modern. Does that mean they are less effective, powerful, or valid? Heck no! These rituals work! That's why after all these decades, people are still performing them.

The reason I bring this up (and suffer the consequences of bursting many-a-folks' bubble of Witchy beliefs) is because of the homogenization and whitewashing of these celebrations and rituals. These rituals work, obviously, but they might not be as effective or impactful for you as an individual with your own practice. Witchcraft needs to connect with *you* and your environment. You should have a physical reaction to magick and be able to see that reflected in your place in the world. That means that for many of us, local magick is where it's at!

Your Role as a Spiritual Leader

Whether you step into leadership in the form of running a coven or Priestexing for larger public events, it's important you understand your impact. As a HP or HPS, you have power and authority over the people in your group. As a public Priestex, you have power and authority over the people who attend the rituals you help facilitate.

If you volunteer to perform an invocation at a public ritual, even if it is for the first time, the participants of that ritual will give you a level of authority. No one attending the ritual will know it's your first time as a public Priestex; they will just see a Priestex helping lead the ritual. And in some cases, participants will assume you have power and authority.

There is a flash and a glamour that comes with being a public Priestex, and this is where the danger lies. If you are drawn toward the role of Priestexing because you want to be "famous," you want people to adore you, or you want power over people, these are not good nor healthy reasons.

Remember way back at the beginning of this book when we talked about *knowing thyself*? When you step into spiritual leadership—either as a teacher, coven leader, HP, HPS, or public Priestex—it is even more vital that you keep doing your personal work.

It's so easy to get caught up in spiritual community politics or using your coven members to strengthen your ego. You have to keep doing your personal work and checking in on why you are holding the roles you are holding. Being a Priestex isn't going to heal your childhood issues; it's not going to make you rich; it's not going to make you a better person. In fact, it is likely to challenge all of those things.

You might think that you are above all that. You don't care about fame or accolades; you don't need or want to be adored. And yeah, that's really good. But you *do* want those things, at least to some degree. Because we all want those things to some degree. The key is to not let those desires be the fuel for your *why*.

When you lose sight of *why* you want to serve your community, then it might be time to take a step back and do some soul searching.

There is a level of responsibility that comes with taking on leadership in the Witchcraft world, and it is important to fully understand that before you get in too deep. As a leader, you will have people that adore you. They might look at you as a teacher, leader, or Priestex that they admire. This can feel really good, fulfilling even. But be careful about believing your own press. Let the accolades help fuel you and keep you going, but don't let accolades inflate your sense of self or your ego.

The pitfalls and challenges of being a coven leader and a public Priestex have a lot in common, but there are also some important differences.

COVEN LEADER

As a coven leader, you will be responsible for the spiritual workings of a small group of people. You will be seen as the authority of the group, no matter your level of experience or expertise. The members of the group will look to you for answers, and to learn what and how to practice.

You can't let this power go to your head. Remember that you are not the ultimate power or authority on the subject of magick and Witchcraft.

As a coven leader, you will have control over who is in your group. You possess a level of gatekeeping power. Not every person is going to "vibe" with you, and there will be aspirants that come a-knocking whom you have no interest in magickally working with.

You need to make sure you have clear guidelines and boundaries about how people are in and out of the group. Be cautious about only accepting coveners that look up to you or adore you; you need a coven that is filled with strong practitioners and Witches, not sycophants.

PUBLIC PRIESTEX

As a public Priestex, you are like a temporary HP or HPS. You might only facilitate one ritual, but those who attend that ritual will see you as the one in charge. They may create all kinds of stories about who you are and your magickal background. Projections at this level of leadership are really high.

You can't let projections go to your head. Some projections will be highly flattering and others, well, not so much. Remember that other people's opinions of you are none of your business—the good ones and the negative ones.

My first year attending Witchcamp I assumed that all the ritual facilitators were professional Witches. I projected all sorts of stories about how spiritual their lives must be. I assumed their full focus and work in the world was Witchcraft. I came to learn later on that out of the ten facilitators at this event, only one of them was supporting themselves as a Witch in community. In fact, one of the facilitators had a prominent job at a tech company in Silicon Valley. He made a lot of money, and that money gave him flexibility to teach about Witchcraft and attend events like Witchcamp. In one conversation, he said it was virtually impossible for someone to make their full living from Priestexing. It was a heartbreaking moment for me because I wanted nothing more than to live my whole life serving as a Priestex.

As a public Priestex, you often have little to no control over who attends your events. There may be people you don't like, people you have personal beef with, or people who have difficult personalities. And that's just too bad for you—there is a ritual to put on. It will be part of your job to hold graciousness and good boundaries when dealing with ritual participants.

THE CIRCLE OF LEADERSHIP

When you step into leadership—whether you choose to take on leadership or it is unceremoniously handed to you—you take on a level of authority and power, and you have a deeper impact on the people around you. These are important powers that any good Priestex should not take for granted. The more responsibility you take on (or is given to you), the more authority you will shoulder. The more authority you have, the more perceived power you possess. The more perceived power you possess, the bigger the impact you will have, for better or for worse. These concepts form the Circle of Leadership.

Authority   *Impact*

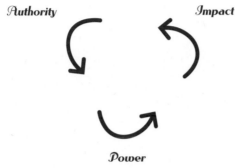

Power

Circle of Leadership

Whether you choose the Priestex life or the Priestex life chooses you, you'll have to determine *why* you are doing it. What is your why? Your why is an important thing to uncover because it will help prevent your ego from getting out of control.

These are healthy reasons for stepping into leadership:

- You want to help people.
- You want to bring people to the Craft.
- Leadership feels like a calling.
- Priestexing feels like the next logical step in your spiritual evolution.
- You want to serve your community.
- You care about the lineage of your tradition carrying on.
- You want to share your knowledge with those starting out on the path.

These are unhealthy reasons for stepping into leadership:

- You want underlings to adore you.
- You want power.
- You want to be seen as a powerful Priestex.
- You are working through negative patterns from your childhood.
- You have a desire to be seen as special and unique.
- You want things to be done your way and only your way.
- You think you have all the answers.
- You want to control others, yourself, or magick.

Authority

When you step into leadership, it gives you an air of authority. This authority may or may not be deserved, and you may or may not be aware of it. But being in leadership comes with people's assumptions and expectations of you.

I once attended a public ritual and was asked, last minute, if I could step in and take on an invocation role; one of the ritual Priestexes had an emergency and wouldn't be able to attend. I agreed and gathered all of the information that I needed to hold my piece of the ritual, but since I hadn't been a part of the planning and setup of the ritual, there were some key pieces I didn't have.

After the ritual was done, a participant came up to me asking questions about the ritual-planning process and how certain aspects of the ceremony had come about. This person thought I was the one "in charge." But that was far from the truth.

This participant had given me a level of authority over the ritual that I didn't actually possess. It was a simple mistake and projection that anyone could have made, but this is one of the pitfalls of public Priestexing.

Rather than try and own this undesired level of authority, I explained my part of the ritual and directed her to someone who could actually answer her question.

POWER

All levels of authority come with differing levels of perceived power. When people see you as an authority, they automatically give you power. Power given to you willingly by others is an authentic form of power. But, as soon as you try to seek out that power or take it from people, it turns into a power struggle, which isn't a form of healthy leadership.

I remember one of the first classes I took with the Reclaiming tradition of Witchcraft. I just assumed that the teachers in the community had all the power—and more than I did. I assumed that they would have all of the answers and know so much more than me.

During a lunch break in a weekend intensive, a fellow student asked one of the teachers a question, and her answer was, "I don't know." It was a question about spiritual concepts that *I* knew the answer to, and the fact that she didn't know the answer left me surprised and a little confused.

She was an excellent facilitator and one of my greatest teachers, but she didn't know everything and she wasn't afraid to admit that. Which is one of the reasons she was such a good teacher.

There are different forms of power when it comes to groups. I wrote about power structures in my book *Witches, Heretics & Warrior Women*:

- **Power-Over:** This is the power structure that most of us are familiar with. This system is one of domination and scarcity. Motivation most often comes from fear. This structure lies to us by suggesting that power is a limited resource. It teaches that only those at the top have power and you must fight your way up the "ladder" to get it—and then continue to fight those behind you to keep it. In this system, everyone is your adversary.
- **Power-With:** In this structure, power is shared. It shows up in relationships and thrives in collaboration. This structure requires respect, support, and empowerment. Power-with makes it possible for differences to keep us together rather than drive us apart. We can function collectively. Power is not a resource that needs to be fought over because when we come together, we have more of it.

• **Power-Within:** This is a solo structure. Power-within has an individual realizing they inherently possess personal power, and therefore, everyone else does too. We each have capacity, we each have worth, and we can each make a difference. When we feel strong in our individual power, we can more easily accept that each person also possesses this power. It's not a competition, it is simply truth. When you have power-within, it is easier to function in a power-with structure. When you have power-within, it is easier to see how power-over doesn't really work.[33]

Impact

When you step into leadership, take on a level of authority, and gain power from those around you, you have to be even more aware of your impact. Your words have power; we know this as Witches. And in a ritual, your words have even more power.

I once attended a public ritual with well over one hundred participants. During the ritual, several Priestexes "drew down" or aspected several different Goddesses. Throughout the ritual, these dozen Priestexes walked around the room, offered blessings, and asked questions of the participants. During the hour-long ritual, not one of the Priestexes came and spoke to me.

This left me feeling unworthy. Of course, this had more to do with my own baggage and what I was going through emotionally and spiritually at the time, but these Priestexes' actions had a huge impact on me. I don't think the intended impact from the ritual planners was for participants to feel isolated.

Scaling the Ritual

A little trial and error can provide you with a lot of information when it comes to putting on rituals. But there are a few standards and tricks that can help you avoid some of the bigger ritual blunders. One key is to attend other folks' rituals.

---

33   LeFae, *Witches, Heretics & Warrior Women*, 80–81.

When you can, attend open rituals, public rituals, and Witchy events. Go to conferences and gatherings where there are a lot of different traditions represented. Go to rituals. Attend ceremonies. When you go as a participant, you get a good idea of what works and what doesn't.

By attending lots of different rituals, you also start to see what traditions are good at what. There are some Witchcraft traditions that do a great job of creating sacred space. There are traditions that do a great job raising energy. There are some traditions that rock at putting on a ritual performance. I've yet to find a tradition that is excellent at all of the things, all of the time.

When you attend rituals from different traditions, you can start to piece together what creates a strong and solid ritual.

SOLITARY/COVEN/GROUP(S)

What works for a solitary, or individual, is vastly different than what works for a small group, or coven, and this is vastly different from what works for a large group. Knowing how to succeed in each of these three different gathering sizes will help your rituals come together more easily.

Solitary

When you do rituals on your own, you don't have anyone else to worry about. The ritual is yours. This might lead you to believe that you can just half-ass it, stop right in the middle to take a wee, or phone it in. Nope, sorry. That's not the case.

As a solitary, you need to make sure that the rituals you create engage *you*. You know what works for you and what doesn't. Or, you should be working to figure all of those things out.

One of the biggest issues with solitary rituals is giving yourself an out or not taking it as seriously as you might if you had other people depending on you. When creating rituals to perform on your own, make sure you create space for mirth and reverence. Do your due diligence to create and craft a rite that is fun, moving, and appeals to your spiritual needs.

Another major issue with solitary rituals is actually performing them. As a solitary, it's easy to just not do the ritual. You might get frozen by not wanting to make a mistake or not being sure what to do. Since it's just you, there is no one that you have to be accountable to. Make sure you do the thing!

As a solitary, you are also the only Priestex of the ritual. That means all the pieces of the ceremony are yours to hold and perform. You might find that your energy burns out more quickly. You might find yourself totally wiped out or with a ritual hangover afterward. If something goes wrong in the ritual, it will be totally up to you to course correct. This can help you grow, but it can also be a harder path to go alone.

There have always been solitary practitioners in Witchcraft, and there always will be. Ultimately, Witchcraft is highly personal and subjective, which perfectly lends itself to people who want to practice their craft on their own.

Coven

A coven is a special thing. And I've come to discover a functioning coven that lasts for years and years is a rare thing. However, no matter how quickly a coven might come into and out of existence, they always serve a purpose.

Covens are a chosen spiritual family, and they allow you to have deep connections with a group of other people. You perform magick together, you step into ritual together, and it is very intimate. The relationship of a coven requires vulnerability.

The amount of people in a coven is typically small. You need at least two people to make a coven and really, the more people you add to the group, the more challenging it gets. I once heard that the reason the number thirteen was considered bad luck was because that was the number of Witches in a coven. Thirteen is actually a pretty great number for a group, but too many more than thirteen and you are asking for issues. More people, more problems.

A coven is like a Witch clique, but hopefully in a good way. The more people involved in a coven, the more likely smaller cliques will develop, and this can create cracks and drama. Covens, just like friend groups and community groups, are full of people. And all people are working on their own stuff. In a coven, personal issues can come up more often than in other types of groups because they are spiritual in nature.

There are some real benefits to being a part of a coven. When you practice as a solitary, the only experience you have is your own. When you practice with a coven, you get the benefit of others' experience. You might have something weird or random happen in ritual and another coven member had that same experience. You get to bounce your experiences and ideas off of other practitioners and you go through magickal experiences together.

Coven work is a magick in and of itself. There is a level of group mind that develops when you really bond with a coven. I've been in coven rituals where we are all clearly thinking the same thoughts and moving like one body. It's not a thing you can truly explain or plan for; it is something that just happens when trust and love are formed.

Plus, with a coven, you have the benefit of many hands making for lighter work. The setup process, the cleanup process, the purchasing and gathering of ritual supplies, and even the doling out of ritual roles—all of these things can be shared among coven members. It takes the pressure off you as a solitary to do everything.

When it comes to planning rituals for a coven, it really depends on what kind of coven you want to be involved with. In the book *The Empowerment Manual* by Starhawk, she writes about the six types of leadership. Her list of leadership types was inspired by Daniel Goleman, who was a pioneer of the idea of emotional intelligence.[34] Based on Starhawk's writing, here are my personal four types of leadership that are best for covens:

- **Visionary:** In this style, the leader keeps their eye on the bigger picture. This group style is best for newer groups. The leader in this style will need to be able to help others focus on the coven's goals and manifest the path ahead.
- **Coaching:** With this leadership style, the person in the role of leader focuses on shaping and developing the skills of the individual members of the group. They are focused on helping coveners face their growing edges.

---

34   Starhawk, *The Empowerment Manual*, 133–34.

- ◆ **Affiliative:** In this style of leadership, the leader is focused on building relationships and getting participants to bond. They know how to best bring people together and create a cohesive group. This style of leadership is great for new groups that need to connect.
- ◆ **Democratic:** The democratic leader takes all folks' ideas and needs into consideration, but ultimately, they make all decisions. They make sure all voices are heard and tend to go with the majority.

TRADITION

If your coven is part of a specific tradition of Witchcraft, there will always be rules on how you run and function. With traditional Witchcraft, it's likely there will be a High Priestess (HPS) and/or High Priest (HP) who will plan, and likely execute, most of the rituals. In traditional covens you will find liturgy for most, if not all, rituals. In most traditional covens, there is less ritual writing or creation.

In a traditional coven, the members are committed and dedicated. There is likely an initiation process that is required for coveners to participate.

ECLECTIC

If you aren't part of a specific tradition, you can set up your coven any way you like. Perhaps there is a hierarchy, perhaps not. If there is set leadership, the ritual planning will mainly fall on their shoulders. If your coven is nonhierarchical, then you might rotate the ritual planners and facilitators.

The members of an eclectic coven might not have a hierarchical leader, but the members are all committed and dedicated to meeting and performing rituals regularly. There may be specific rules on how you get involved with the coven and what makes you an official member.

In an eclectic coven I was part of, we would plan our schedule of gatherings for the year ahead in January. Then we would draw two names from a hat for each month, and those two folks would plan that month's ritual. This worked really well because there was always a rotation of leadership and we each got to work closely with a rotation of other members of the coven.

In a more eclectic style coven, you need to have clear agreements on how the group functions in order to keep things fair and balanced. One issue that may come up is participants not feeling empowered to speak their minds. Encouraging participation from all coven members is vital for the health of an eclectic coven.

You may also need clear boundaries on formal roles within the coven. Even in a group with no or rotating leadership, there needs to be a process in place. The more processes you have in place ahead of issues cropping up, the less likely there will be issues that blindside your group.

Roles in a coven could be things like a treasurer, a record keeper, someone to monitor supplies and get them when needed, someone to remind folks of upcoming gatherings and supplies to bring, etc.

Here are some things to consider about leadership:

- What are the roles in your coven?
- Who currently holds these roles, and how often will they rotate?
- What is the process of stepping into, or out of, these roles?
- Are there limits on how many roles one coven member can hold at one time?
- Is there a training or transition process for roles moving from one covener to another?

FREEFORM

A freeform coven is also unattached to a specific tradition and offers the most flexibility of all the options. With a freeform coven, there may be a larger number of members; people will attend gatherings when they feel called, but there isn't any level of commitment.

In this style of coven, none of the rituals are planned in advance. At each gathering there is a moment of connection and sinking into intention, but the rituals are allowed to unfold in whatever manner happens at the time of the gathering.

LARGE GROUP

When I say large group ritual, I am talking about a ritual with more than two dozen participants. The more people at a ritual, the more complicated the facilitation becomes. I've facilitated rituals for twenty-five people, and I've been part of a facilitation team for two thousand. The nuts and bolts of these two group sizes actually have a lot more in common than not. The biggest thing to remember is the more participants, the more Priestexes you need to help with the group energy.

There is nothing like the buzz and power that comes from a large group ritual. Every summer I attend an event through the Reclaiming tradition of Witchcraft called California Witchcamp. Witchcamps happen all over the world, and I've been blessed to attend quite a few of them, but the one in California is my home camp.

It is a weeklong intensive in the woods. All of the food is provided, and you stay on-site for the week. Everyday there are workshops, and every night there are rituals. I've attended this event as a camper and as a teacher/facilitator. Every year there are about one hundred Witches that attend California Witchcamp. The rituals at this event are always amazing, transforming, and powerful. It's what keeps me returning year after year.

Big rituals are powerful because the larger the number of people participating in a ritual, the more energy can be built. The power raised in a solitary ritual will never match the power raised in a ritual with one hundred people.

But the larger number of people involved, the more ritual wrangling you have to do. You can't just stand in the middle of the space and read a ritual off a sheet of paper. In large rituals you have to engage the participants and bring a lot more theatre and performance art into the ritual.

Here are some things to keep in mind with big group rituals:

- Folks need something to do; standing around and listening to other people go on for too long will get boring.
- Breaking the ritual into pieces where there are different modalities (like dance, trance, storytelling, etc.) helps keep people with different learning styles engaged.

- Be prepared for feedback.
- There are a lot more space and sound logistics to deal with.
- There are a lot more physical needs to deal with and accommodate, including mobility issues.
- Being too elaborate can trip you up, just as much as keeping it too simple can. You have to find a sweet middle ground of simplicity and complexity.
- You might have to shift your plan mid-ritual. With a large group, you have to follow the flow of energy, and that might lead away from what you originally wanted to do.

There are skills that come with facilitating large rituals. You might even consider these Priestexing skills. You can read all about them and gain a certain amount of knowledge, but really these skills are best developed by practicing. Doing is going to give you so much more awareness and information than reading.

As a Priestex, there are levels of awareness you need to hold during a ritual for a group that you don't have to worry about when leading a ritual on your own. In a group ritual, you need to have:

- Awareness of your body and gestures and how they will impact the participants.
- Engagement with the intention of the ritual and the magickal energy as it unfolds.
- Connection to the participants. Look people in the eyes, move around the space, turn and face different directions.
- Knowledge of the flow of the ritual beyond "your part." If you are doing just one invocation, know who is stepping up before you and after you.
- Connection to the outline of the ritual, the engagement of the participants, and the flow of magickal energy, all at the same time.
- Awareness that what the group does or experiences is much more important and empowering than what the participants might see

you do. You are not the star of the show—you are a facilitator of the process.

RITUAL FEEDBACK

In many Witchcraft circles, there isn't a lot of room for feedback, and I think that is a major issue. In hierarchical traditions, the HPS and HP create rituals or lead the rituals, and rarely have I seen any requests made for feedback in groups like this. However, as ritual planners and creators, getting feedback for rituals we put on, or our specific roles in those rituals, provides a ton of valuable information on how to improve ourselves for the next ritual.

And in saying that, not all feedback is created equal. If you attend a ritual and you didn't like it, ask yourself *why* you didn't like it. Can you take a step back and figure out what didn't work for you and what you might have done differently? Is the dissatisfaction you have connected to your own personal triggers, growing edges, or blocks, or is it connected to something in the ritual planning and setup that could have been done better?

Feedback isn't bitching about a ritual or tearing a Priestex down. It is an opportunity to lift Priestexes up and empower ritualists to try again and in a different way. Here are some tips on giving feedback:

- ◆ **Think about your motives.** Is this a personal issue, or is there something bigger going on?
- ◆ **Ask permission.** Right after the ending of a ritual might not be the best time to tell a Priestex that their role didn't work for you. That Priestex might be in their own grounding process, or beating themselves up for a mistake, or in post-ritual bliss. You don't want to be the one to burst their bubble. Instead, ask if they are open to feedback. They will say yes or no. They might also say yes, but later. And conversely, if you are the Priestex being asked if you are ready to hear feedback and you're not, it is totally okay to say no.
- ◆ **Offer feedback in a timely manner.** If you attend a Samhain ritual and spot some ritual issues, don't wait until the next year's Sam-

hain ritual to offer that feedback. About a week out from a ritual is a good time to offer feedback.

- **Remember that feedback can be positive too.** You might think that feedback is only connected to problems, issues, mistakes, or errors, but it's not. Feedback can also be sharing what worked really well, what impressed you, or what was transformative. People need to hear what works as well as what didn't.

- **Be specific.** "The ritual was boring" isn't helpful feedback. "There were too many silent moments; singing or music would have helped hold my attention better" is a much better piece of feedback because it points to exactly what was lacking.

- **Speak for yourself.** There is nothing more deflating than hearing feedback presented from one person, but referred to as coming from "several of us." People need to be willing to offer their own feedback in their own words. You might think you are speaking for a group of people, but don't. If everyone agrees with you, they need to be brave enough to share their feedback on their own.

- **Offer suggestions.** In a previous example, the feedback suggested that music or singing would have helped the ritual work better for the participant. Providing a tangible suggestion for how the ritual could have been different helps ritualists see other options for the next time.

- **Check yourself.** Remember that feedback should be offered to help someone grow their Priestexing skills. Why are you offering feedback in the first place? Are you being kind? Can you say the words in a way that is kind and compassionate?

Rituals Where You Are

Much of modern Witchcraft practices are based on European history, seasonality, and regionality. If you live in Mexico, the Pagan Wheel of the Year from modern practices doesn't really make a lot of sense. In fact, just the regional differences from Northern California to Southern California are different enough that it could feel like you are in a different world. Why should we all celebrate the turning of the Wheel in the same way?

Homogenization of Witchcraft practices might make us feel like we *have to* celebrate the winter solstice in front of a roaring fire, hiding indoors from the snow and cold weather. The Yule holiday might bring forth a prescribed image of praying for the sun to return so we don't starve to death. But where I live, it can be just as warm and sunny on the winter solstice as it is on the summer solstice. Plus, I don't have a fireplace, and I can just go to the grocery store to fill my coffers for the winter. Right? Rather than try and fit an ancient regional and seasonal holiday into my California landscape, I'm better off creating a cycle of celebration that fits where I live.

The first step in creating a cycle of celebrations for your own practice is to have a relationship with where you live. This requires you to pay attention to the shifts in weather, animal migrations, local celebrations, and subtle changes in your area.

Knowing these things about your home environment is deep Witchcraft, and it is truly based on ancestral practices, because our ancestors all over the world were creating their practices based on where they lived and what was going on in their environment.

Moons

One way to expand your exploration of place is by connecting with the lunar phases. Nothing is more classic than the image of Witches dancing around in the moonlight. But why do we care about the moons, and how do we best create rituals to honor the moon's cycles?

FULL MOONS

Also referred to as *esbats*, full moon rituals are very common in Witchcraft circles. However, how the full moon is worked with varies greatly.

No doubt you've heard some of the moon names that get thrown about every month. Labels like "Beaver Moon," "Pink Moon," "Cold Moon," etc., get attached to the full moons at different times of the year. Some of these names come from agricultural history, some of them are Anglo or Germanic in origin, and some come from different Indigenous tribes in North America.

When I say that the January full moon was called the Wolf Moon, that was actually referring to the monthlong period of time from the full moon in January until the next full moon in February. It can be a little confusing to look at the lunar phases in combination with our modern calendar because they are literally two different ways of tracking time. But when we look at the moons this way, we can see that a full moon has a larger impact than just one day on the modern calendar—the names and energies of the full moon are a message for the month.

To add more confusion into the mix, tracking time lunarly means the Wolf Moon we typically associate with the month of January might actually happen in late December or early February. Again, keep in mind that the lunar calendar runs on a different timeline than the Gregorian calendar that most of the modern world uses.

The names for the full moons are not universal concepts, and at the very worst, they are culturally appropriative.[35] Many of the Native names that have been ascribed to the full moons gained popularity on a larger scale after they were published in a farmer's almanac in the 1930s.[36] Although calling the January full moon the Wolf Moon might be an ancient practice for Indigenous people, non-Native folks using those labels is relatively new.

And there are more issues with these terms. Again, I live in Northern California, so the name "Snow Moon" doesn't align with anything I experience in real life at this time of the year. Why would I call the full moon a Snow Moon when it never snows here? How can I have a relationship with the power of the Snow Moon when that is not my lived experience?

These names are arbitrary. Keep in mind that all of these names are focused on the Northern Hemisphere, and more specifically, northeastern North America. Although the full moon can be seen by the whole planet,

---

35   "Full Moon Names for 2022."
36   Johnston, "Moon Missive."

the names that have become popular in modern Witchcraft really only apply to a small percentage of the population.

Here are some of the names for full moons that many have adopted into their practice in modern Witchcraft. Please note, I am using time frames and descriptions based on the Northern Hemisphere. When it is the spring equinox here, it is the fall equinox in the Southern Hemisphere, and vice versa.

January

The full moon in January happens when the moon is in the astrological sign of Cancer or Leo.

- **Wolf Moon:** In an old farmer's almanac, it was written that at this time of the year you can often hear wolves howling at night. It's possible this has Anglo-Saxon origins, or it could have originated with the Native tribes of New England; it is uncertain.[37]
- **Center Moon:** The Assiniboine people of the plains of North America used this term for the January full moon because it was in the center of their winter season.[38]
- **Other January Full Moon Names:** Quiet Moon, Snow Moon, Cold Moon, Chaste Moon, Disting Moon, Moon of Little Winter.[39]

February

The full moon in February happens when the moon is in the astrological sign of Leo or Virgo.

- **Snow Moon:** Called this due to the snowy conditions in northern North America, especially in New England. This name comes from the Algonquin people and describes what is going on at this time of the year in this part of the world.[40]

---

37   Georgiou, "What Is a Wolf Moon?"
38   Georgiou, "What Is a Wolf Moon?"
39   Conway, *Moon Magick*, 19.
40   Johnston, "Moon Missive."

- **Hunger Moon:** This name likely also originates from the Native communities of New England. It's not hard to imagine why hunger would be associated with this time of the year, when produce is scarce.[41]
- **Other February Full Moon Names:** Ice Moon, Storm Moon, Horning Moon, Wild Moon, Red and Cleansing Moon, Quickening Moon, Big Winter Moon.[42]

March

The full moon in March happens when the moon is in the astrological sign of Virgo or Libra.

- **Worm Moon:** Named because in some places, this is when you start to see earthworms emerge from the earth after the cold winter.[43]
- **Lenten Moon:** This is an old Anglo-Saxon term and has a relationship to the Christian celebration of Lent. The following full moon would land on Easter.[44]
- **Other March Full Moon Names:** Seed Moon, Plow Moon, Sap Moon, Crow Moon, Moon of Winds.[45]

April

The full moon in April happens when the moon is in the astrological sign of Libra or Scorpio.

- **Pink Moon:** This moon is named for the pink phlox flowers that are in bloom at this time of the year and are native to North America.[46]

---

41 Johnston, "Moon Missive."
42 Conway, *Moon Magick*, 41.
43 Johnston, "Moon Missive."
44 Johnston, "Moon Missive."
45 Conway, *Moon Magick*, 61.
46 Johnston, "Moon Missive."

- **Egg Moon:** This is Anglo-Saxon in origin and refers to the time of the year when the wild birds begin to lay their eggs.[47] This could also be loosely associated with the mythology of the Germanic Goddess Eostre.
- **Other April Full Moon Names:** Growing Moon, Planting Moon, Budding Trees Moon, Hare Moon.[48]

May

The full moon in May happens when the moon is in the astrological sign of Scorpio or Sagittarius.

- **Flower Moon:** For much of the world, in the month of May flowers are in bloom. It makes sense that the name would relate to what is blossoming. It is believed that this name is Algonquin in origin.[49]
- **Milk Moon:** This is an Anglo-Saxon term. The belief is this term came into use to describe the time of the year when weeds and plants were abundant and milk-producing animals had plenty to eat, and therefore, plenty of milk was being made.[50]
- **Other May Full Moon Names:** Bright Moon, Frog Return Moon, Planting Moon, Merry Moon.[51]

June

The full moon in June happens when the moon is in the astrological sign of Sagittarius or Capricorn.

- **Strawberry Moon:** This term comes from the Algonquin, Ojibwe, Dakota, and Lakota peoples. This is the time of the year that wild strawberries become ripe.[52]

---

47   Johnston, "Moon Missive."
48   Conway, *Moon Magick*, 77.
49   Backlund, "A Milk Moon Is Coming."
50   Backlund, "A Milk Moon Is Coming."
51   Conway, *Moon Magick*, 95.
52   Gregory, "When to See the Full 'Strawberry Moon.'"

- **Hot Moon:** It's not hard to understand why June would be connected to heat. This is the month of the summer solstice in the Northern Hemisphere, and in many places, the height of warmer months happens at this time.[53]
- **Other June Full Moon Names:** Rose Moon, Mead Moon, Honey Moon, Strong Sun Moon, Lovers' Moon.[54]

July

The full moon in July happens when the moon is in the astrological sign of Capricorn or Aquarius.

- **Buck Moon:** Named for the time of the year when the antlers of the deer begin to emerge. Likely originates from the Algonquin people.[55]
- **Hay Moon:** This name is Anglo-Saxon and connects to the time of the year that the first grain harvest would take place for most Germanic peoples.[56]
- **Other July Full Moon Names:** Thunder Moon, Wort Moon, Blessing Moon, Moon of Blood, Fallow Moon.[57]

August

The full moon in August happens when the moon is in the astrological sign of Aquarius or Pisces.

- **Sturgeon Moon:** This name originated with the Native peoples from around the Great Lakes and Lake Champlain. August is the best month for sturgeon fishing.[58]

---

53   Gregory, "When to See the Full 'Strawberry Moon.'"
54   Conway, *Moon Magick*, 115.
55   "July Full Moon."
56   "July Full Moon."
57   Conway, *Moon Magick*, 135.
58   Kettley, "Full Moon 2020 Meaning."

- **Grain Moon:** Again from the Algonquin people, this was the time of the year when the harvests for grain would begin.[59]
- **Other August Full Moon Names:** Corn Moon, Barley Moon, Dispute Moon, Green Corn Moon, Fruit Moon.[60]

September

The full moon in September happens when the moon is in the astrological sign of Pisces or Aries.

- **Harvest Moon:** September marks the fall equinox and the time of harvest for the majority of the Northern Hemisphere.
- **Corn Moon:** This month is an integral point in the harvesting of corn. Again, this has North American origins, mainly from Plains Native tribes. This is also the name for the August full moon for other Native tribes.[61]
- **Other September Full Moon Names:** Wine Moon, Singing Moon, Rutting Moon, Falling Leaves Moon.[62]

October

The full moon in October happens when the moon is in the astrological sign of Aries or Taurus.

- **Blood Moon:** This name relates to the increase in hunting during the month of October as ancient cultures prepared for the coming winter. There is often an eclipse at this time of the year that is referred to as the Blood Moon.[63]
- **Hunter's Moon:** It is at this point of the year that the focus really turns to winter preparation. Hunting would increase in order to make sure there was enough meat to make it through the months ahead.[64]

---

59   Kettley, "Full Moon 2020 Meaning."
60   Conway, *Moon Magick*, 151.
61   "July Full Moon."
62   Conway, *Moon Magick*, 169.
63   "July Full Moon."
64   "July Full Moon."

- **Other October Full Moon Names:** Shedding Moon, Harvest Moon, Falling Leaves Moon, Freezing Moon, Ice Moon.[65]

November

The full moon in November happens when the moon is in the astrological sign of Taurus or Gemini.

- **Frost Moon:** This label likely comes from the fact that frost regularly appears in northern North America during the month of November, as the weather becomes even colder.[66]
- **Beaver Moon:** In the northern parts of North America, this is the time of year that beavers focus on preparations for the upcoming winter and retreat inside. It is a sign that we humans need to start doing the same.[67]
- **Other November Full Moon Names:** Dark Moon, Fog Moon, Mourning Moon, Mad Moon, Oak Moon.[68]

December

The full moon in December happens when the moon is in the astrological sign of Gemini or Cancer.

- **Cold Moon:** Winter solstice takes place during the month of December. This is considered to be the peak of winter and one of the coldest months of the year.
- **Moon Before Yule:** This term is Anglo-Saxon and refers to the Northern European celebration of the winter solstice.
- **Other December Full Moon Names:** Oak Moon, Wolf Moon, Long Night's Moon, Big Winter Moon.[69]

---

65 Conway, *Moon Magick*, 189.
66 "July Full Moon."
67 "July Full Moon."
68 Conway, *Moon Magick*, 229.
69 Conway, *Moon Magick*, 247.

Blue Moon

The blue full moon can happen at any time of the year and in any astrological sign. There are actually thirteen full moons every calendar year. By simply looking at the math, you can see that one of our modern months will have two full moons in it. This second full moon in one month is referred to as a blue moon.

NEW MOONS

New moons don't tend to have the same attention paid to them as full moons do. Although, from a Witchcraft perspective, new moons hold just as much power and potential as full moons. The names for the full moons were mainly picked by different Indigenous tribes of North America and were used to describe a month of time. According to this system of tracking time, the new moon is only one moment that happens during the time between full moons. Many modern Witchcraft practitioners have turned to astrology to name the new moons.

Just like full moons happen on a monthly basis, so do the new moons. From an astrological perspective, the new moon will always be in the astrological sign that the sun is in that month. The new moon is a good time for self-reflection, setting intentions, and beginning new projects.

New Moon Names

- **January:** Capricorn or Aquarius.
- **February:** Aquarius or Pisces.
- **March:** Pisces or Aries.
- **April:** Aries or Taurus.
- **May:** Taurus or Gemini.
- **June:** Gemini or Cancer.
- **July:** Cancer or Leo.
- **August:** Leo or Virgo.
- **September:** Virgo or Libra.
- **October:** Libra or Scorpio.
- **November:** Scorpio or Sagittarius.
- **December:** Sagittarius or Capricorn.

Each of the astrological signs contains a different energy and power. This will impact the best use of the energy of each new moon, and it changes every year. Tracking the new moons and when they fall will need to be done on a monthly basis.

- **Aries:** Independent and action-orientated.
- **Taurus:** Stabilizing and grounding.
- **Gemini:** Communicative and curious.
- **Cancer:** Sensitive and caring.
- **Leo:** Expressive and creative.
- **Virgo:** Discerning and thoughtful.
- **Libra:** Social and likable.
- **Scorpio:** Intense and penetrating.
- **Sagittarius:** Adventurous and positive.
- **Capricorn:** Enduring and reserved.
- **Aquarius:** Intellectual and insightful.
- **Pisces:** Intuitive and creative.[70]

You can use the traditional astrological energy of each new moon to help you determine how to best utilize that power in your rites.

✦ *Home Adventures* ✦

What do all of the full moon names have in common? They all describe what is happening to the land, the animals, and the beings at certain points in time. These names show a human awareness of what is going on in the world around us. We need to reestablish these connections.

What do all of the new moon names have in common? They all describe what is happening from a cosmic perspective. We also need to reestablish these connections.

---

70   Nicholas, *You Were Born for This*, chap. 3.

Now it is your turn to create names for the full moons and new moons based on your location and practices. Here are some ways to do this:

+ Track the full and new moons, and use words that reflect what is changing in the natural landscape where you are located.
+ Pay attention to the astrology of the full and new moons, and allow these names to influence the titles you choose.
+ Create rituals and/or celebrations to honor each of these moons.
+ Get together with other Witches and share your connections and feelings about the moon's cycles.

Sabbats

The Wheel of the Year, as most modern Witches know it, has been heavily influenced by Western and Northern European cultures. Just like the labels for the full moons, they don't always relate to where we are located on the globe. Traditionally, the Wheel of the Year was a cycle that moved from the two solstices and two equinoxes, also called the quarters, with the midway points, or cross-quarters, between each of these four points in time.

The solstices and equinoxes are astrological or planetary moments. They are moments when there are shifts happening on our planet due to the earth spinning on its axis around the sun. The solstices mark the points of peak light and peak darkness, while the equinoxes are the points of balance in light and darkness.

Here is an explanation of the Wheel of the Year and the sabbats as most modern Witches recognize them.

SAMHAIN

Typically celebrated on October 31 or November 1 in the Northern Hemisphere and on April 30 or May 1 in the Southern Hemisphere. Sometimes referred to as the Witch's New Year. It is a time to celebrate our dead and honor our ancestors. In Wicca, Samhain is when the Old God dies and the Crone mourns for him. It is a time when harvests are ending and preparations for winter need to be well underway. It is believed that the "veil between the worlds" is the thinnest at Samhain and Beltane, and it is easier for us to send and receive messages from the Otherworlds.

WINTER SOLSTICE

The actual date of the winter solstice will vary from year to year, but it tends to fall around December 21 in the Northern Hemisphere and June 21 in the Southern Hemisphere. The winter solstice is the shortest day of the year. It is a time to sing to the sun and call that energy back. It is a time to practice hibernation magick and look at what needs to go underground for the rest of the winter. Many celebrants stay up all night to sing to the sun in the morning. In Wicca, this is the moment when the Oak King is at his weakest as the sun begins to grow again. The Goddess gives birth.

IMBOLC

Typically celebrated on February 1 in the Northern Hemisphere and August 1 in the Southern Hemisphere. Imbolc is the first breath of spring. It is the moment when the long winter begins to shift and warmer days are ahead. Often this holiday is connected to the Irish Goddess Brigid, and many rituals are held in her honor. It is a time of setting intentions for the year and making sacred pledges. Imbolc is when baby animals are born and milk flows. In Wicca, this is when the Goddess becomes the bride.

SPRING EQUINOX

The actual date of the spring equinox will vary from year to year, but it tends to fall around March 21 in the Northern Hemisphere and September 21 in the Southern Hemisphere. It is a time of balance when the light and the dark are equal. The height of the year is ahead. This is a time of celebrating fertility; eggs play a large role in this. Decorating eggs, hiding eggs, and seeking eggs are all pretty traditional parts of the Equinox. The spring equinox is loosely connected to the Germanic spring rites from the Goddess Eostre. In Wicca this is when the Goddess and God begin courting. And the battle of the Oak King and Holly King happens, with the Holly King winning to control the rest of the year.

BELTANE

Typically celebrated on May 1 in the Northern Hemisphere and November 1 in the Southern Hemisphere. Beltane is the peak of spring energy. It is a time of sexuality and fertility. The flowers are in bloom, the bees are buzzing, and everything feels alive. It is traditional to dance around a Maypole at Beltane as a spell for fertility. It is also a time of cleansing with fire by jumping over a bonfire (or balefire) and making commitments to relationships for the year ahead. In Wicca, the Goddess and the God come together in sexual union at this time.

SUMMER SOLSTICE

The actual date of the summer solstice will vary from year to year, but it tends to fall around June 21 in the Northern Hemisphere and December 21 in the Southern Hemisphere. On modern calendars this date is called the "first day of summer"; it is actually the peak energy of summer. The summer solstice is when we want to be outside. It is warm, the sun is shining, and we can almost forget winter even exists. It is the height of sun magick. The summer solstice is a good time to have a bonfire and release old things that no longer serve. This includes journals, spell supplies, and habits you want to let go of. In Wicca, this is the time when the Holly King is at his weakest as the year rolls forward.

LUGHNASADH

Typically celebrated on August 1 in the Northern Hemisphere and February 1 in the Southern Hemisphere. Lughnasadh, also called Lammas, is the first harvest. It is a celebration that food exists and there will be more of it. It's traditional to bake bread at this time of the year and work spells into the dough. Lughnasadh is connected to the Celtic God Lugh, as you might discern from the name of the holiday. That connection is why folks will often play games of skill on this day, and it's not unusual to have flea markets or craft fairs. In Wicca, the Goddess is pregnant and begins to quicken.

FALL EQUINOX

The actual date of the fall equinox will vary from year to year, but it tends to fall around September 21 in the Northern Hemisphere and March 21 in the Southern Hemisphere. The fall equinox is also referred to as "harvest home" and is considered the second harvest. This is when the shift from growing to reaping really comes into play. The energy shifts from warmth and summer to darkening and deepening as winter moves ever closer. In Wicca, the Oak King and Holly King battle again, with the Oak King winning the fight.

THE WHEEL OF THE YEAR

As you can see, our planet is always in spiritual balance as it moves through the Wheel of the Year. When it is the spring equinox in the Northern Hemisphere, it is the fall equinox in the Southern Hemisphere. This awareness has radically shifted the way I relate to the Wheel of the Year.

The moment of peak energy on one side of the world is a moment of deepening energy on the other. Therefore, we as a planet always remain in balance. This also shifts the way that I look at holidays like Beltane and Samhain, which are in opposition to each other from a planetary perspective. Samhain is a celebration of death and Beltane is a celebration of life. Of course they should be connected by their polarity.

The Wheel of the Year has been a part of modern Witchcraft for close to one hundred years. It is a lovely practice and it is one that most modern Witches are familiar with. But it is so connected to the histories of Europe that it leaves a lot to be desired.

The solstices and equinoxes are literally points in time that impact our planet. They are traceable and trackable movements of growth and decline. It makes sense to mark these moments and honor the shifting of the cycles.

However, just like the full moons, the cycle of shifting seasons is very different depending on your location. Rather than focus your Wheel of the Year on the harvest cycle of Western Europe, how about creating a Wheel of the Year that connects to what is happening where *you* live?

I'm not saying you have to throw the whole Wheel of the Year concept out the window, although if you want to do that, go for it. What I am saying is there is a way to make the Wheel more connected to your personal magick, not just something invented several decades ago.

Once upon a time (like the 1980s and 1990s), there was a need and a desire to unite Witches and Pagans. Especially in the United States, we needed legitimacy and unifying concepts to connect us. We needed to be safe from losing our jobs or our children for practicing the Craft. These are still important things across the world, but in the United States we are no longer on a PR campaign to gain legitimacy in the overculture. It's less important to have homogenization—in fact, I would say that homogenization we worked to create decades ago is starting to cause harm.

Now we need Witchy folks, coven leaders, solitaries, and magicians to take back the control of their practices. We need to weave in threads of our *actual* communities and physical locations in order to make our practices stronger and more powerful.

This year, I encourage you to take note of what is going on during the Wheel of the Year where you live. For example, what works best for me based on where I live is looking at the seasonal holidays as more of a "tide" of time, rather than just one single day. There is an ebb and flow to energy and seasonality. These tides aren't specific dates or moments on the calendar, but are fluid like the tides of the sea.

In my annual tracking, Samhain-tide flows from the fall equinox to the end of the calendar year, right around winter solstice.

This leads into Brigid-tide. Which flows from the beginning of the calendar year, or winter solstice, through to Beltane.

Then it moves into Lammas-tide. This energy goes from Beltane through to the fall equinox.

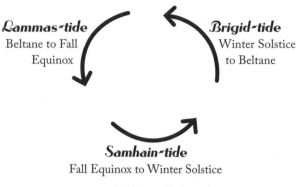

Lammas-tide
Beltane to Fall
Equinox

Brigid-tide
Winter Solstice
to Beltane

Samhain-tide
Fall Equinox to Winter Solstice

Sabbats—Tides

These "tides" are central to the ebb and flow of where I live and might not work for other places in the world. Your mileage may vary. I highly encourage you to figure out what the flow and tides might be for your life and area.

In my little corner of the world, one of the signs that we have moved into Brigid tide is the growing of daffodils. They always seem to poke out of the ground during the transition from one tide to the next. And at the opposite end of the year, around Lammas and the fall equinox, the flowers we call naked ladies appear. They are a herald that the tide is shifting and that the seasons are on the move.

✦ Home Adventures ✦

To start the work of connecting with place, get a journal. If you'd like to use a current Book of Shadows, that's fine, but I highly recommend getting a grimoire that you use just for tracking your land. This could be a paper journal, a three-ring binder, or an electronic collection of notes. The vehicle for tracking isn't important—what is important is the tracking.

Every new moon and full moon, take out your grimoire and write down what is happening in your landscape. Use one whole page for each new and full moon, even if you only write a couple of sentences; you'll want to return to this same event the next year.

Here are some things to make note of in your grimoire:

+ The day of the week.
+ The weather patterns that have been happening the week leading up to the moon phase.
+ What plant life is growing or receding.
+ What local events are happening, like a Founder's Day celebration or a local annual street fair.
+ How you are feeling emotionally, physically, and spiritually.
+ Anything you have noticed from animal life in the week prior to the moon phase. (Your house pets count as animal life!)
+ The time of sunrise and sunset.
+ The time of moonrise, moonset, and moon phase.
+ How close you might be to one of the traditional Wheel of the Year Pagan holidays.

Once you've gone through a whole year, repeat the process for a second year. Write down the notes for year two right under year one on the same page. This will help you start to see patterns in what is going on around you.

Connecting to the land you live on, deepening your relationship to the cycles where you are, and being part of the flow is probably the most important magick that any Witch can do.

Finding Your Daily Practice

Rituals aren't just the thing you do on the full moon or winter solstice. Rituals happen every day, in small moments and in your everyday activities. Your daily spiritual practices are the rituals that help fuel your magick between the bigger rituals you might perform on special events. Creating a daily practice full of rituals you love and enjoy will help your continuous work of knowing thyself.

Your daily practice is really just three simple things:

1. It's yours, so it needs to appeal to you.
2. It's something that you need to do every day.
3. It's a practice, not a perfect, so don't be afraid to mess it up.

A daily practice is important because it helps you stay present. It is easy to get caught up in our goals and where we are going. It is easy to worry about what is to come and the things on our schedules. It is also easy to stress over the mistakes we've already made. It is easy to stew on the wrong things we said or did in the past.

The things from the past are done. The things from the future we can't control. The present moment is all that we have. When we are present, we are calm and aware and, well, here, now.

PRACTICES TO BRING YOU TO YOUR CENTER

It is important for our physical, mental, and spiritual health to take time for ourselves every single day. It is good for our development as Witches and our basic humanity. Now, I understand this is a hard task. I've worked a full-time job with three kids, a husband, five pets, and a house that was falling apart. I know when you have lots of responsibilities, it is hard to add something that might feel like another task to your list. And yet, it is important.

If there is a way to change your morning or evening routine to give you time and space, do that. If there is a way to take your lunch break and go for a walk outside, do that. If there is a way for you to delegate, shift responsibilities, or change some of your circumstances to make more room for spiritual pursuits, do that.

Mindfulness and spiritual gurus will often encourage people to get up earlier in order to create the time needed for spiritual practices, and if that fits in your life, do it! However, I'm not a morning person *at all*. Telling me to wake up thirty minutes earlier to do a daily practice means I won't do that daily practice.

Be realistic about who you are and how you live your life. You don't have to totally transform who you are and how you go about your business—unless that's needed. And only you can determine if that is the case.

Stepping into Witchcraft means work. And work requires a certain level of commitment. Make the commitments that you can right here and now.

Daily ritual practice can look a lot of different ways. Here's a list to get you started.

Journaling

Giving yourself time every day to write is a powerful practice. You can set boundaries around journaling by either assigning a set number of pages or minutes for you to write. You don't have to have a prompt or specific topic; just let yourself write freely. Allow whatever needs to come out to be written on the page.

As has been noted before, when it comes to journaling, you can use notebooks, three-ring binders, or electronic means of recording your thoughts and experiences. Do what works best for your life.

At least once a month (and even better if the moon is full), go back and read your pages. Pay attention to threads of consistency, patterns, or other interesting notes.

Meditation

There are lots of forms of meditation. One might work better for you than another, but you have to try a practice for at least a couple of weeks before you will be able to determine if it is a good match for you or not.

- **Mindfulness:** This is the form of meditation that most people think of when they hear the word *meditation*. The technique is Buddhist in origin. It is a practice of watching your thoughts without any attachment to them. This is often combined with breathwork.
- **Focused:** This form of meditation utilizes one of the five senses. This might look like moving prayer, mala beads through your fingers, counting your breaths, watching a candle flame, or listening

to music or chimes. You tune out all other thoughts and stimulation and just focus.

- **Movement:** As you might imagine, this form of meditation is movement based. Practices like Qigong are forms of movement meditations. Typically, these are gentle and slow movements so you can be present with your mind and your body at the same time.
- **Mantra:** This process utilizes the repeating of a spiritual phrase, chant, or prayer. This might be done in conjunction with running prayer beads through your fingers.
- **Relaxation:** This is a combination of physical and mental processes. Every muscle is tightened and then released. This allows you to sink into a deep state of relaxation.
- **Visualization:** This form of meditation is best done with a voice leading you through a guided exercise. There are many recordings and YouTube videos that offer guided visualization meditations.

Grounding and Centering

If you go back to "Step Two: Grounding and Centering," there are some prime examples of grounding and centering exercises.

When I teach these concepts in my classes, I encourage my students to practice different forms of grounding at different times of the day. Ground in the morning when you first wake up. Ground in the evening before sleep. Ground during your lunch break. Ground before going into a difficult or challenging meeting. Ground after having a difficult discussion. Ground when you have anxiety or are particularly stressed. Test out grounding at all of these different times to determine which works best for you.

Physical Exercise

There is a lot to be said for exercise. Movement is a great daily practice to help you stay connected with your body. The good news is there are tons of ways to move your body. This isn't about weight loss or muscle mass; it *is* about having a healthy relationship with your body. If the idea of going to the gym fills you with dread, don't worry! Here are some ways to incorporate exercise into your day-to-day.

- Swimming.
- Dancing.
- Yoga.
- Stretching.
- Walking.
- Pilates.
- Circuit training.
- Weight lifting.
- Jogging.
- Hiking.
- Team sports.

Breathwork

Breathing might not seem very spiritual. It is something that we do all the time without having to think about it. But the *way* we breathe can shift our awareness, bring a sense of calm, and help our thought processes in a variety of ways. Breathing with intention and focus is very powerful.

There are many types of breathwork, and they all have the potential to do different things. Try these out and see which feels the best for your body. As with all daily practice, it is important to know what type of breathwork helps you relax or calm down *before* you feel anxious or stressed. If you haven't tested breathwork ahead of a stressful time, you won't think to use it when you are in a stressful time.

- **Box Breathing:** Exhale slowly to clear your lungs. Inhale to the count of four and then hold to the count of four. Exhale to the count of four and then hold to the count of four. Continue this process for as long as possible.
- **Diaphragm Breath:** Sit upright with your shoulders relaxed. Inhale into your belly through your nose until you can't take in any

more air. Purse your lips and exhale slowly through your mouth. Repeat this process until you feel your energy shift.

- **4-7-8 Breath:** Hold your tongue to the roof of your mouth, pressed against the back of your top teeth. Inhale through your nose to a count of four. Hold your breath to the count of seven. Exhale through your mouth, making a sound, to the count of eight. Repeat this pattern for at least four full breaths.

- **Alternate Nostrils Breath:** Sit with your back straight. Exhale completely and then use your right pointer finger to close your right nostril. Inhale through your left nostril and then close your left nostril and open your right. Exhale completely through your right nostril and then inhale through your right nostril. Then plug your right nostril and open your left. Repeat this process for five minutes.

- **Circular Breathing:** Inhale and then exhale without allowing a pause between the breaths. Keep going for several minutes. (This type of breathwork can make you dizzy or lightheaded, so be cautious.)

PRACTICES TO CONNECT YOU TO THE DIVINE

For many modern Witches, our relationships to deities, nature spirits, and divinity is a big part of how and why we are Witches. When I use the word *divine*, I mean a large number of things. Divinity might mean deities. The divine could be that ineffable thing in the universe that binds us all together. The divine could also be referring to your own God-self. Divinity could be physics, dark matter, or something else. All of these things are true.

No matter how you view the divine, it is power for your magickal and spiritual practice to be in relationship with that energy.

Just like connecting with your center requires time, connecting with the divine requires some of your time too. The good news is you can add these two practices together!

Connecting with the divine doesn't have to be a long or drawn-out process that you have to go and seek out. One of the concepts I write about in my book *Walking in Beauty* is the fact that there is beauty and awe around us all of the time. Connecting to the power of awe is connecting to divinity. It is all around us, all the time. It is in us, all the time.

I do have a daily practice of connecting with my specific deities, but I also have a magickal practice of seeking beauty, and this also is part of my divine practice. Every day—and I mean that, every single day—there is some moment that leaves me breathless or in awe about the world (in a positive way). Today, as I was driving my cat to the vet, I saw a beautiful hawk sitting right on the top of a stop sign. The majesty of the bird, the perfection of that moment, left me smiling and feeling blessed.

Daily practice, daily ritual, is that simple. By setting a daily goal or intention to seek out the divine, you will. It could be through a spiritual practice, or it could be through seeing majesty in the world around you.

There are numerous ways to add daily rituals of working with the divine into your day. Here are some ways to get you started.

Devotionals
If you are a polytheist or work with any deities, devotionals should be part of your practice. Devotionals don't have to be long or complicated. You could burn incense, leave food or drink, play music or chant, or tidy up their altar space. Devotionals are the acts of care and service that you give to your Godds to show them you care about the relationship.

Go Outside
This might seem too simple, but seriously just go outside. Go and sit in your backyard for ten minutes. Take a walk to a local park and sit. Open one of your windows and sit with the air hitting your face. Put your bare feet on some grass or touch your hands to the ground. Give yourself a moment to remember the world is so much bigger than you.

Commune
Sit down with your Godds and just be. Allow yourself to simply talk or to listen. You don't need to plan anything or force a specific interaction. Just commune.

Walk in Beauty

In the morning, set an intention that you will find some moment where you will be awestruck by something in the world. You don't have to work hard for this to happen. Just pay attention. Allow the beauty of the world around you to unfold and leave you feeling blessed.

PRACTICES THAT HELP DEVELOP A NEW SKILL

Part of spiritual growth comes from learning new things. It doesn't matter how long you've been practicing, there is always more to learn and explore. I've been a practicing Witch for nearly thirty years and I still work to expand my skills and learn new things. Just like we can never stop learning from a mental perspective, we will never stop learning from a spiritual one.

Sometimes this part of the daily practice can feel like the most exciting. When you are learning a new skill, you might be more inclined to want to do that practice first because it is new and interesting. And other times, this part of your daily practice might feel scary, hard, frustrating, or too challenging.

I learned to read runes by making them a part of my daily practice. It was hard and sometimes frustrating, but I really wanted to have a relationship with the runes, so I set out the time and intention to do it.

Just like the other parts of your daily practice, you have to make room for this in your life. But unlike the other parts of daily practice, this one might take more time and focus. If you want to learn to play the flute as a devotional to Apollo, you will need more than five minutes every day to really master that new skill.

This part of your daily practice might require a bit more dedication and commitment from you. You may have to schedule time in your day to make sure it happens. Don't let yourself feel daunted by the task. Instead, look at it as a great adventure that you can't wait to engage in!

There are many skills that can be added to your magickal repertoire. Here are a few ideas to get you started.

Divination

Learning a new form of divination is a fun new skill to practice as a daily ritual. Different forms of divination are like learning a new language; it will take time to become proficient.

- Pull a tarot card every day and read what the booklet that came with the deck says about that card's message.
- Pull a rune every day and read about it in a book about runes.
- Pull out a book and do some bibliomancy.
- Throw some bones or curios and do a reading about the day ahead.

With any form of divination, you can do a reading for the day ahead and see what comes from it. Check in at the end of your day to see how the messages manifested.

Rotate this practice. For one week, perform a divination first thing in the morning as a way to get messages about the day ahead. And then, the next week, do a divination right before bed as a way to help you process the day you've had.

Music

Learn to play an instrument, practice your singing, or put music on and let it move your body. Music can be played as an act of devotion to your deities or as a meditation practice. Music helps shift our mood and bring our emotions to different places. You can also choose music that you find magickal, spiritual, or energy-altering in order to allow music to impact your daily practice.

PUTTING THE DAY IN DAILY

There are daily practices that you can add into your regular routine that might not appear spiritual on the surface. Take a moment to look at some of the activities you do every day. Is there a way for you to bring ritual (or at least spiritual awareness) into these activities?

For example, I make a cup of black tea every morning. While the kettle is heating up, I grab my mug and tea bag. Throughout this process, I hold an intention for the day ahead. I breathe deeply, expressing gratitude for my life. When the water is hot, I pour it into my mug with the intention that I will have a day filled with blessings and joy. If there is a specific goal or spell I'm working, I will also draw symbols or sigils over the top of my cup before drinking.

There are also a handful of pills and vitamins that I take on a daily basis. When I take my pills, I do so with gratitude for my health and well-being. Sometimes this is a long internal process; sometimes it's just a simple speaking of the words "Thank you" out loud and then swallowing the pills.

A friend of mine uses her first morning urination as a way to clean out negative energy. She recites a mantra that as she releases the urine from her body, she also releases all that no longer serves.

You might choose specific music or audiobooks to listen to on your daily commute as a way to connect more deeply with your spiritual self.

My partner cooks our family meals way more often than I do, and it is part of his daily practice. He focuses his intention on love and health and directs it into the meals he prepares. He uses kitchen tools that have been charged and blessed for magickal purposes. Cooking and eating are part of his daily practice.

At my Witchcraft shop, we all have specific prayers that we recite in the morning when we open up the doors. And we have certain gratitude practices that we do in the evening when we close up.

Gardening is an excellent daily practice. It allows you to connect with the land and the earth. Taking care of plants helps people stay focused and calm. And it helps you connect more deeply with where you are.

We all have things we do every day, like brushing our teeth or feeding the cat, that we don't associate with our spiritual lives. But the truth of the matter is everything you do is a part of your spiritual life, because you are a spiritual being. Bring more awareness of that into the seemingly mundane parts of your life.

✦ *Home Adventures* ✦

Look at the things that you do every day. Mentally go through your typical day, from the moment you wake up to the moment you lie down to sleep. Write a list of all the routines and activities you always complete, even when you don't have the bandwidth or the desire to do them.

When you have a nice list of at least a dozen items (you're likely to have a lot more than that), pick out three. Then ask yourself, *How can I incorporate more spiritual connection into these tasks?* Write down the first answer that pops into your head.

See if you can implement at least one of these practices immediately.

Ritual Checklist, Ritual Outlines, and Sample Rituals

This section contains sample ritual outlines and a ritual checklist to help you start crafting your own rituals that actually work. These are just frameworks to get your own creative juices flowing. There are some suggestions for ritual workings to perform during the body of the rite, but the rest of the outline is left as just bullet points to give you the chance to try out different ways of performing invocations and different ritual pieces.

At the end of this section, I have also included several useful sample rituals for daily practices and other common needs.

Ritual Checklist

Here is a form that you can use when planning rituals. It will help you determine the step-by-step process and give you a place for all your ritual notes and ideas. This ritual checklist is also a guideline so you don't miss any important parts or pieces of crafting great rituals.

This outline lists all the pieces of ritual that you'll find in most modern Witchcraft rituals. However, feel free to leave out or cross out those pieces that won't be included in a ritual that you are crafting. Again, this is a jumping-off point for you to create your own magickal rituals.

Initial questions to answer:

+ Who is this ritual for?

    _____

    _____

+ What do you want participants to have or know after the ritual is
  completed?

    _____

    _____

    _____

    _____

    _____

+ What skills are needed to create this container?

    _____

    _____

    _____

    _____

    _____

+ What physical tasks need to be completed during the rite?

    _____

    _____

    _____

    _____

    _____

+ Who is Priestexing this ritual?

    _____

    _____

RITUAL INTENTION:
◇ Cleansing Modality:
 Name of Priestex Performing:

◇ Grounding Modality:
 Name of Priestex Performing:

◇ Casting Modality:
 Name of Priestex Performing:

◇ Air Invocation Style:
 Name of Priestex Performing:

◇ Fire Invocation Style:
 Name of Priestex Performing:

◇ Water Invocation Style:
 Name of Priestex Performing:

◇ Earth Invocation Style:
 Name of Priestex Performing:

◇ Spirit Invocation Style:
 Name of Priestex Performing:

◇ Deity(s):
 Name of Priestexes Performing:

◇ The Fae:
> Name of Priestex Performing:

_____

◇ Ancestors:
> Name of Priestex Performing:

_____

◇ Descendants:
> Name of Priestex Performing:

_____

◇ Other Ally(s):
> Name of Priestex Performing:

_____

◇ Body Working Modality:
> Name of Priestexes Performing:

_____

◇ Raising Energy Modality:
> Name of Priestexes Performing:

_____

◇ Cakes and Ale:
> Name of Priestex Performing:

_____

◇ Musical Needs:

_____

◇ Setup:

_____

◇ Cleanup:

_____

SUPPLIES NEEDED:

◇ _____

◇ _____

◇ _____

◇ _____

◇ _____

◇ _____

◇ _____

◇ _____

◇ _____

◇ _____

◇ _____

◇ _____

◇ _____

◇ _____

◇ _____

◇ _____

◇ _____

◇ _____

◇ _____

◇ _____

◇ _____

◇ _____

◇ _____

◇ _____

◇ _____

◇ _____

◇ _____

◇ _____

Sample Ritual Outline for Devotion

- Creating Intention
- Cleansing
- Invocations
- Deity Calling
- Working
  - Create an altar for your devotional.
  - Sing, chant, make music, burn incense, give food, make offerings.
  - Ask for help.
  - Sit in silence and see what messages come through.
  - Have a party in their honor.
  - Perform divination.
- Energy Raising
- Devocations

Sample Ritual Outline for Spellwork

- Creating Intention
- Cleansing
- Invocations
- Working
  - Candle magick.
  - Potion making.
  - Create a charm or mojo bag.
  - Set up an altar for ongoing spellwork.
  - Charge an object.
  - Make an amulet or talisman.
  - Perform a ritual bath.
  - Create a crystal grid.
- Energy Raising
- Devocations

Sample Ritual Outline for Self-Care

- Creating Intention
- Cleansing
- Invocations
- Working
    - Sit in meditation.
    - Take a cleansing bath.
    - Go for a walk in a beautiful place.
    - Anoint yourself with oil.
    - Get a massage.
    - Eat a delicious meal.
    - Dance.
    - Journal.
    - Cry/laugh/emote/express.
- Energy Raising
- Devocations

Sample Ritual Outline for Seasonal Celebrations

- Creating Intention
- Cleansing
- Invocations
- Working
    - **Samhain:** Create an ancestor altar, have an ancestor feast, toast to your beloved dead, trance to the isle of apples, carve pumpkins.
    - **Winter Solstice:** Create and burn a Yule log, have a secret Santa gift exchange, do a meditation about going deep into the winter earth, stay up all night and sing up the sun, decorate a Yule tree or individual stockings, light candles to remember the warmth of the sun.
    - **Imbolc:** Make pledges for the year ahead, renew and charge your ritual tools, cleanse your home, self, and ritual spaces.

- ¤ **Spring Equinox:** Decorate hard-boiled eggs, hide and find decorated eggs, have a picnic outdoors, plant seeds with magickal intentions.
- ¤ **Beltane:** Erect a Maypole and dance around it, make flower wreaths to wear and decorate ritual space, jump over bonfires.
- ¤ **Summer Solstice:** Have a bonfire, burn old ritual implements or journals, be outdoors in the sunshine.
- ¤ **Lughnasadh:** Bake bread with ritual intention, have a feast, play games of skill, make a corn dolly or effigy and burn it, reset wards and shields.
- ¤ **Fall Equinox:** Have a feast, celebrate your harvests, dedicate the last harvested grain or vegetable to the divine, organize a food drive.
- ◆ Energy Raising
- ◆ Devocations

A Ritual to Start Your Day

As soon as you wake up in the morning, before even opening your eyes, take a deep and intentional breath. Say the following words out loud:

Today will be a glorious day. I am grateful for this day.

Sit up and put your feet on the floor. Give yourself some time to ground and connect with the energy of the earth. Drink a small glass of room-temperature water. (Ideally, this will be left out the night before.) As you drink, feel the water permeate your body. Feel the water molecules hydrate the cells of your body.

From this point, you might want to add in a meditation or breathwork practice. You might take some time to journal or perform some slow and gentle movement. When you are finished, go about your day.

A Ritual to Close Out Your Day

At least thirty minutes before you get into your bed, do a calming practice. This could be a meditation or breathwork activity. This might be journaling or slow and steady movement. Once this is complete, get into your bed.

Lie down and connect with your body. Let your awareness scan your body. See if you can notice any areas of discomfort or stuck energy. If you come across any areas like this, breathe into them and offer them love and blessings. Say the following words out loud:

Today was a glorious day. I am grateful for this day.

Shift your awareness to focus on your breathing until you fall asleep.

Daily Blessing Ritual

This ritual can be performed at any time of the day. I find it is best done at the start of the day or before stepping into a ritual.

SUPPLIES

- Dried rosemary
- Charcoal incense burner
- Firesafe container
- Lighter

SETUP

Place the firesafe container on a heat-resistance surface. Light the charcoal so it gets hot. When ready, put the dried rosemary on the top of the charcoal.

RITUAL

Ground and center yourself in your favorite way. Take time to come to a place of focus and presence.

As you complete the following process, visualize the smoke clearing out negative energy and cleansing both you and the physical space you are in. Use the smoke of the incense as a cleanse for your body and spirit.

Hold up the incense burner, facing the north, and use the smoke to draw a pentacle in the air in front of you. Turn to the east and use the smoke to draw a pentacle in the air in front of you. Repeat this process to the south, and to the west. Return to the north and draw a final pentacle in the air to complete the circuit of cleansing.

Speak out loud to any guides or allies that you would like to watch over your day. Speak from the heart, asking for their guidance and support. Ask for blessings for your day.

Say:

> *Cleanse this space and bless this day.*
> *Keep all negative forces at bay.*
> *I walk in strength and beauty.*
> *I walk in magick and mystery.*
> *May I be of service to the land.*
> *May I allow the flow of magick from my hand.*

Breathe deeply until you feel ready to move on. Put out the burning herbs and go about your business.

Protection Ritual

This is a ritual to charge an amulet for protection. Pick a piece of jewelry that will be comfortable for you to wear every day. This could be a ring, necklace, pendant, bracelet, anklet, or even a pair of earrings. The piece of jewelry you pick shouldn't be too flashy; choose something that will blend in and fit with any style of clothing you might wear.

SUPPLIES
- Selected piece of jewelry
- Athame
- Dragon's blood incense
- Black glass-encased candle
- Bowl of water
- Palm-sized stone

+ Small bowl of salted water
+ Protection anointing oil

SETUP

Place all of the ritual supplies on your altar space. If you feel so inclined, you can add an altar cloth, flowers, or other decorations you feel called to add. Make sure the piece of jewelry is in the center of the altar space.

RITUAL

Before stepping into ritual space, ground and center yourself until you feel fully present and ready to step into your rite.

Pick up the athame, pointing it at the ground. Breathe in and pull up iron energy from the earth into your blade. When you feel as though your tool is full of the power of iron, face the north and send that energy out to the edge of your ritual space. Direct the energy out while drawing an invoking pentacle.

Turn to the east. Continue to send the iron power out. Draw an invoking pentacle. Repeat this, turning to the south, the west, and back to the north. Point your tool above you and draw an invoking pentacle. Finally, point your tool below you and draw the final invoking pentacle.

Step up to your altar and place your athame back on it. Light the incense. Holding the incense in one hand, turn to the east with your arms raised above you. Breathe in deeply and connect to the element of air. Say:

> *I call upon the powers of the air.*
> *I call forth your wisdom and intellect.*
> *I call forth your clarity and song.*
> *Hail and welcome.*

Lower your arms. Return the incense to the altar. Light the candle. Holding the candle in one hand, turn to the south. Raise your arms above you. Breathe in deeply and connect to the element of fire. Say:

> *I call upon the power of the fire.*
> *I call forth your energy and connection.*

I call forth your transformation and creativity.
Hail and welcome.

Lower your arms. Return the candle to the altar. Pick up the bowl of water and turn to the west. Holding the bowl in both hands, raise your arms above you. Breathe in deeply and connect to the element of water. Say:

I call upon the power of the water.
I call forth your flow and intuition.
I call forth your depth and understanding.
Hail and welcome.

Lower your arms. Return the bowl of water to the altar. Pick up the palm-sized stone, holding it in one of your hands, and turn to the north. Raise your arms above you. Breathe in deeply and connect to the element of earth. Say:

I call upon the power of the earth.
I call forth your strength and focus.
I call forth your resolve and grounding.
Hail and welcome.

Lower your arms and return the stone to the altar.

If there is a specific deity that you want to call into your ritual to ask for their protection, do this now. Speak from the heart and call them into your ceremony.

Step up to your altar and pick up the piece of jewelry. Sprinkle it with the salted water, cleansing the item of any impurities or negative energy it may have been carrying. Visualize any negativity melting away.

Run the piece of jewelry through the incense smoke and say, "By the power of air."

Run the piece of jewelry quickly and carefully through the candle flame and say, "By the power of fire."

Sprinkle the piece of jewelry with the water from the bowl you used to invoke water and say, "By the power of water."

Hold the piece of jewelry to the stone and say, "By the power of earth." Hold the jewelry in your dominant hand and lift it up to the sky. Say:

Blessed is this (name of item) with the powers of the elements.
Blessed is this (name of item) with the powers of protection.
When I wear this (name of item), I will be protected from all harm.

Anoint the jewelry with your protection oil. Visualize the item being charged with protection energy. As you do this, call upon your guides, allies, or any specific deities you invited into the circle to aid in creating protective power for your jewelry.

Put the piece of jewelry on and feel, visualize, and imagine yourself being cloaked in protective energy.

When you feel ready, speak words of gratitude to your guides, allies, and any specific deities that you may have called into your ritual. Briefly speak your gratitude to each of the four elements that you called in.

Pick up your athame. Point it to the ground and draw a banishing pentacle. Point your athame above you and draw a banishing pentacle. Turn to the north and draw a banishing pentacle. Turn to the west and repeat the process. Do this again to the south, to the east, and then again to the north.

The rite is complete.

Anointing Ritual

This ritual is best performed before stepping into ceremony, before performing divination, or prior to any moment when you want to shift your consciousness into a more spiritual state of being.

SUPPLIES
- Favorite anointing oil
- Bowl of salt
- Shower
- Fluffy towel
- Full-length mirror

SETUP

You will need to take a shower and afterward, have access to the towel, oil, and mirror.

RITUAL

Take the bowl of salt with you into the shower and give yourself a nice scrub. As you scrub, focus on cleansing your spirit body as well as your physical one. Pay close attention to your heart space and your throat. Don't forget the back of your body as well.

When finished, step out of the shower and dry yourself off. Do this slowly and with the intention of cleansing and refreshing your energy.

Stand in front of the mirror and use the anointing oil to bless yourself. Put a drop of the oil on your finger and touch it to the bottoms of each of your feet. As you do this, say, "Bless my feet for walking in strength."

Place a drop of oil right below your navel and say, "Bless my body for being an expression of life."

Place a drop of oil in the center of your chest and say, "Bless my heart for love and connection."

Place a drop of oil on your throat and say, "Bless my voice for speaking truth."

Place a drop of oil on your third eye and say, "Bless my vision for knowledge and faith."

Finally, rub the remaining oil on your fingers into your hands, focusing on the palms of your hands. Say, "Bless my hands that do the sacred work."

You are now ready to step into your rite or ceremony.

Money Drawing Ritual

Perform this ritual when you need to shift your financial luck. This rite isn't for calling in a specific sum of money, but rather for shifting your financial situation long term. This ritual may need to be performed several months in a row, and occasionally afterward going forward. This ritual is best performed during a full moon.

SUPPLIES
- Three green chime candles and holders
- Two-dollar bill
- Abundance oil
- Lighter
- Dried, chopped peppermint

SETUP
Have all of the ritual items set up on an altar space.

RITUAL
Cleanse, ground, and center yourself in your favorite ways. When you feel ready, cast a circle around your ritual space in your favorite way.

Step up to your altar and anoint the two-dollar bill with abundance oil. This is best done by putting a dot of oil in each corner of the bill and right in the center, creating a five-spot pattern. Set the bill in the middle of your altar space.

Next set the three green candles around the bill, forming a triangle with the bill in the middle. Light the candles. Sprinkle the peppermint over the entire altar space. Be at your altar while the candles burn and focus on wealth and abundance flowing swiftly and easily to you. Feel yourself filled with prosperity. If you need to step away, make sure the candles are burning in a safe environment and don't leave them unattended for long.

When the candles are finished burning, take down the ritual circle that you created.

Place the two-dollar bill in your wallet and give it as part of a tip next time you receive service. Gather up the peppermint and sprinkle it across your front door.

Health Ritual

This ceremony is for ongoing health and wellness. It is a good ritual to perform when there is an illness "going around" your school or workplace, or during cold and flu season. This is an ongoing type of rite that you will want to keep performing until you are clear from the bug.

SUPPLIES

- White glass-encased candle
- Blue permanent marker
- Dried nettle
- Health sigil
- Wand
- Lighter

Health Sigil

SETUP

Copy the health sigil for reference. Put all of the ritual objects on the altar for the ritual working.

RITUAL

Cleanse, ground, and center yourself in your favorite way.

Pick up the wand and hold it to your heart. Breathe and focus on health, healing, and wellness. When you feel ready, face the north and begin to create a protective barrier around your ritual space. Turn in a clockwise direction, pausing when you reach the east, south, and west, then return to the north. Point the wand above you, filling the above with healing energy. Point the wand below you, filling the below with healing energy.

If there are any specific allies, guides, or deities that you want to call into your ritual, do that now.

Step up to your altar. Pick up the blue marker and draw the health sigil on one side of the glass candle. On the other side of the glass, write the names of everyone who will be included in this working; this might include all members of your household or family.

Sprinkle the top of the candle with a pinch of nettle.

Hold the candle in your hand and fill it with healing energy. Visualize a blue glowing energy flowing through your hands and into the candle. Allow this to continue until it feels like the candle is full of healing power. Take a deep breath and blow more of the healing energy into the top of the candle.

Tap the candle on your altar surface three times, then light the candle.

Don't formally take the circle down, but rather allow the healing energy you have built up to slowly dissipate in your space.

Keep the candle burning for as long as you can without leaving it unattended. If you have to step away, extinguish the candle, but relight it as soon as you can. Once the candle has burned through, repeat the process.

Keep this ritual going until you've made it through the sickness.

Calling In a New Lover Ritual

Perform this ritual when you are ready for a new relationship. This is not a ritual for a specific target. It should come from a place of openness when you are ready for the right person to come into your life.

Before starting the process of calling in a new love, make sure that you are clear of any old loves. I highly recommend taking a black walnut bath and allowing yourself to scream and cry to release anything old that is hanging on.

Once you have done the work of releasing, you can begin the next step of the process.

PRE-RITUAL WORK

Get a pink glass-encased candle and a sheet of paper. Light the candle and spend some time pondering the qualities of your ideal partner. Be honest and specific without being too closed off to potential and mystery. Think about age ranges, their history with marriage and/or children, and their thoughts on future marriage and/or children. Consider how far away they might live. Consider all of the potential boundaries you need to be happy in a relationship.

When you have a nice solid list, set it aside for a full week.

After a week, pull the list back out and look over what you've written. See if any adjustments need to be made. Allow this process to take the time it needs. If you want to work on your list for a few weeks, that's okay. Remember, this is to call in a new lover—make it a good one!

Once your list is done, perform this ritual on the next full moon. This ritual needs to be performed in a bathroom.

SUPPLIES

- Your list of qualities
- Two red chime candles in holders
- Pink altar cloth
- A handful of rose petals in a bowl
- A handful of damiana leaves in a bowl
- A teaspoon of honey
- Love oil
- Pink thread
- Lighter or matches
- A bathtub
- A tool that you can use to carve into the candles

SETUP

Lay out your altar cloth. Place all of the other ritual items on the altar in a way that is pleasing to you. Make sure the two candles are close to each other.

RITUAL

Ground and center yourself. Take some time to focus on love and relationships. Connect with your heart center and allow it to fill with a glowing golden light. Feel yourself full and surrounded with love energy.

When you feel ready, step up to the altar space and sprinkle the rose petals and damiana leaves across the altar cloth. Take one of the red candles and carve your name and birthday into the wax. On the other candle, carve the words "my perfect love."

Anoint each of the candles with the love oil, then roll them in the herbs that you've sprinkled on the altar space. Put each of the candles back into their holders and move them as close together as possible. Put your list of qualities under the candle you have carved for your perfect love. Use the pink thread to wrap the two candles together.

Light the candles. As you do, say:

> *I am ready for love.*
> *I call in my perfect love.*
> *I am ready to love.*
> *I call in my perfect love.*
> *By the power of the rose.*
> *By the power of the flame.*
> *I call to my match.*
> *And I know they seek the same.*

As the candle burns, begin to fill up the bathtub. As the water rises, scoop up the rose petals and damiana leaves and sprinkle them into the bathwater. Take a taste of the honey and say:

> *Like bees to honey.*
> *My lover seeks me now.*

Pour the rest of the honey into the bathwater. Get in and soak. Know that your love is headed to you. Stay in the warmth of the bath until the candles have burned out. This may take some time. If you feel so called, bring yourself to orgasm and use that energy to complete the spell.

When the candles have burned out, get out of the tub and dry off. Anoint yourself with the love oil and roll up the entire altar in the altar cloth. Place it under your bed until your desire has come to pass.

Meditation Ritual

This is a simple ritual that can be performed daily or as needed.

SUPPLIES

+ Time
+ Space

SETUP

Find a comfortable place to sit where you will be undisturbed for at least ten minutes.

RITUAL

Once you are seated in a comfortable place, ground and center yourself. Take some deep breaths and allow yourself to come to stillness.

Perform one of the meditation practices from "Step Five: Action." After ten minutes, see if you want to continue or if you feel complete. If complete, go about your day.

Conclusion

Ritual is an important part of life. It is not something we can optionally engage in; it is something we need for our health and vitality. Rituals help bring us a deeper awareness of how we are doing. Rituals help us connect with something bigger than ourselves. And they can provide us with the time and space to heal our hearts, find our power, and become better people.

Rituals are life.

Unfortunately, we don't get a lot of training on how to best perform rituals and incorporate them into our day-to-day lives. Our overculture doesn't exactly recognize the power of ritual or even acknowledge that rituals exist. Our friends and families might have weird preconceived notions of what rituals are. We may have to find support for our ritual lives outside of our regular connections.

Although rituals are our birthright and we inherently know how to perform them, good rituals do take practice. They require a certain level of skill and knowledge. But the good news is, just like any skill, it can be learned.

Whether you perform rituals in large groups, small covens, or on your own, what is important is that you *are* performing rituals.

And it's important to remember that rituals can be simple. We perform so many rituals in our daily lives. There is already a lot of magick right at our fingertips, and we don't have to go about life blindly disconnected from that magick. We can take control and awaken to the flow of magick already around us. We can find daily rituals that feed our minds, bodies, and spirits.

Let your daily life be filled with rituals. Let your daily life be filled with Witchcraft.

Ultimately, remember that Witchcraft is a practice. It is something you have to *do*.

So go forth and do Witchy things!

Acknowledgments

This book would not exist if it had not been for my years of Priestexing in the Reclaiming tradition of Witchcraft. I am grateful to all of my teachers and my teacher's teachers from this tradition. Crafting rituals and holding group magick is something Reclaiming Witches do really well. It is with the deepest respect and humility toward the Reclaiming tradition that I wrote these words. Thank you to all of my teachers, their teachers, ritual facilitators, and community members that have come in and out of my life in the last thirty years. I am so grateful.

Thank you to Heather Greene, Nicole Borneman, and all the other amazing beings at Llewellyn for taking another chance on my words.

Thanks to Tempest for writing the foreword of this book. I am grateful and humbled. Thanks for being a friend.

To Jason Mankey, thanks for the encouragement to keep going.

To Trinity: thanks for creating sigils for me; thanks for being an amazing human.

To Copper Persephone and Diana MelisaBee, who saw something special in me and encouraged me to step forward into leadership. I wouldn't be doing half of what I'm doing if it wasn't for the two of you; thank you so much.

To my beloved Gwion Raven. Thanks for your constant support and cheerleading. You totally believe in me a million times more than I do. You are totally the best in the biz.

Pollyanna Costa, astrologer, magician, and right-hand woman. My life would not be the same without you in it. Thank you so much for all you do to keep my world running. I'm so grateful to you.

Resources

Substance Abuse Resources
SAMHSA National Helpline: 1-800-662-4357

LGBTQ+ Resources
The Trevor Project: 1-866-488-7386

Gay, Lesbian, Bisexual, Transgender National Hotline: 1-888-843-4564

GLBT National Youth Talkline: 1-800-246-7743

Trans Lifeline: 1-877-565-8860

Suicide Prevention Resources
National Suicide Prevention Lifeline: 1-800-273-8255

OTHER SERVICES
National Domestic Violence Hotline: 1-800-799-7233

National Sexual Assault Hotline (RAINN): 1-800-656-4673

Glossary

aether: The fifth element, also referred to as spirit.

allies: Spiritual helpers, guides, and guardians. They may be human, animal, plant, Fae, deity, or other.

altar: The place where you perform magick, do ritual, or have devotional space.

ancestors: Those that have come before you; may be of blood or spirit.

aspecting: Allowing a deity to share your human body.

athame: A ritual knife, typically with a double-sided blade.

aura: The energy field around your physical body.

auric field: See *aura*.

banishing: Releasing or sending energy away.

bell: A tool for ritual, used for shifting energy.

Beltane: Pagan holiday celebrated on May 1 in the Northern Hemisphere and August 1 in the Southern Hemisphere.

besom: A ritual broom, typically used for cleansing.

boline: A curved ritual knife, typically used for cutting herbs.

Book of Shadows: A book of collected spells and rituals, sometimes also called a grimoire.

broom: See *besom*.

cakes and ale: Also known as cakes and wine. Refers to the part of the ritual where food and drink may be served or shared.

casting: The part of the ritual when a sacred circle is drawn to keep the magick being performed safe and contained.

cauldron: A ritual tool for burning, purifying, or transforming ritual supplies.

center: One of the five sacred directions.

chalice: A ritual cup; typically used for libations.

cleansing: A practice of clearing the nonphysical body of negative energy.

consecrate: To ritually make an object sacred for ritual uses.

coven: A group of witches that gather for ritual and magick.

cross-quarters: The points on the Wheel of the Year that fall between the solstices and equinoxes.

deosil: Clockwise.

devoke: To release energies or entities that were called into a ritual circle.

divination: The use of a tool (like cards, runes, bones, etc.) to tune in and listen to your intuition.

elements: Earth, air, fire, water, and sometimes spirit; considered to be the four, or five, sacred elements on the planet.

elementals: The guardians of each of the elements.

energy raising: The point in ritual when energy is raised to activate the ritual or spell.

equinox: Pagan holidays. There are two: The spring equinox is on March 21 in the Northern Hemisphere and September 21 in the Southern Hemisphere. The fall equinox is on September 21 in the Northern Hemisphere and March 21 in the Southern Hemisphere.

espurging: A cleansing practice that uses salted or blessed water and herbs on the skin.

etheric body: See *aura*.

grimoire: See *Book of Shadows*.

grounding: The practice of shaking off distractions and being fully present in the moment.

initiation: The ritual practice of spiritually committing to a lineage Witchcraft tradition.

invoke: The point in ritual when allies and supporting energies or entities are called into the circle.

Lammas: See *Lughnasadh*.

Lughnasadh: Pagan celebration that takes place on August 1 in the Northern Hemisphere or March 1 in the Southern Hemisphere, also referred to as Lammas.

mirror: A ritual tool for sending, receiving, or trapping energies.

pentacle: A ritual tool representing the element of earth. Used for grounding and charging.

quarters: The Pagan holidays of Samhain, Beltane, Imbolc, and Lughnasadh. Also, a term for the four directions or four elements.

Samhain: Pagan holiday that takes place on October 31 in the Northern Hemisphere and May 1 in the Southern Hemisphere.

sigil: A magickal symbol.

solitary: A Witchcraft practitioner that practices on their own, without a group.

solstice: Pagan holidays. There are two: the summer solstice is on June 21 in the Northern Hemisphere and December 21 in the Southern Hemisphere. The winter solstice is on December 21 in the Northern Hemisphere and June 21 in the Southern Hemisphere.

spirit: See *aether*.

spirit body: See *aura*.

staff: A ritual tool used to send or direct energy and to represent the crossroads.

stang: A ritual tool used to represent the crossroads of the Witches.

sword: A ritual tool representing the element of air. Used to send, direct, or cut energy.

Theban script: A magickal alphabet often used to keep spells or ritual writings a secret.

wand: A ritual tool representing the element of fire. Used to send or direct energy.

ward: A magickal protection that is set up to keep a space safe.

watchtower: The location of the guardians of each of the elements in each of the four directions.

Wheel of the Year: The modern annual Pagan cycle of seasonal holidays.

widdershins: Counter-clockwise.

wildcraft: The practice of gathering sacred herbs for magickal use.

Bibliography

Backlund, Roya. "A Milk Moon Is Coming and It's the Symbolic Start to Summer You've Been Waiting For." *Elite Daily*, May 24, 2018. https://www.elitedaily.com/p/the-milk-moon-meaning-will-infuse-your-world-with-peace-harmony-9186572.

Benjamin, Esme. "Cleaning and Renewal Rituals from Around the World." *Culture Trip*, April 18, 2019. https://theculturetrip.com/asia/articles/cleaning-and-renewal-rituals-from-around-the-world/.

Blake, Deborah. *The Witch's Broom: The Craft, Lore & Magick of Broomsticks.* Woodbury, MN: Llewellyn Publications, 2014.

Conway, D. J. *Moon Magick: Myth & Magick, Crafts & Recipes, Rituals & Spells.* St. Paul, MN: Llewellyn Publications, 1995.

Coolman, Robert. "Origins of the Days of the Week." *Live Science*, May 7, 2014. https://www.livescience.com/45432-days-of-the-week.html.

Cunningham, Scott. *Cunningham's Encyclopedia of Magical Herbs.* St. Paul, MN: Llewellyn Publications, 1985.

———. *The Complete Book of Incense, Oils & Brews.* St. Paul, MN: Llewellyn Publications, 1989.

Fortune, Dion. *Psychic Self Defense.* York Beach, ME: Red Wheel/Weiser, 1997.

"Full Moon Names for 2022." *Almanac*, January 26, 2022. https://www.almanac.com/full-moon-names.

Georgiou, Aristos. "What Is a Wolf Moon? The Meaning Behind the Name of January 2021's Full Moon." *Newsweek*, January 25, 2021. https://www.newsweek.com/full-wolf-moon-name-january-2021 -1564224.

Glenn, Lori. "Limpias – Energetic and Spiritual Cleansing." American Botanical Council, October 15, 2014. http://herbalgram.org/resources /herbclip/herbclip-news/2014/limpias-energetic-and-spiritual -cleansing/.

Gregory, Christine. "When to See the Full 'Strawberry Moon' and the History Behind It." Rochester First, June 23, 2021. https://www .rochesterfirst.com/weather/weather-blog/when-to-see-the-full -strawberry-moon-and-the-history-behind-it/.

Greenleaf, Cerridwen. *The Witch's Guide to Ritual: Spells, Incantations, and Inspired Ideas for an Enchanted Life.* Coral Gables, FL: Mango Publishing, 2020.

Johnston, Gordon. "Moon Missive: The Next Full Moon Is the Worm Moon, Crow Moon, Crust Moon, Sap Moon, Sugar Moon, or Lenten Moon." Moon: NASA Science, February 27, 2018. https://moon.nasa .gov/news/43/moon-missive-the-next-full-moon-is-the-worm-moon -crow-moon-crust-moon-sap-moon-sugar-moon-or-lenten-m/.

"July Full Moon." The Nine Planets. Updated November 3, 2020. https:// nineplanets.org/july-full-moon/.

Kettley, Sebastian. "Full Moon 2020 Meaning: Why Is the August Full Moon Called the Sturgeon Moon?" *Express.* Updated August 4, 2020. https://www.express.co.uk/news/science/1318131/Full-Moon-2020 -meaning-August-Full-Moon-name-Sturgeon-Moon.

Knight, Shauna Aura. *Ritual Facilitation: Collected Articles on the Art of Leading Rituals.* Self-published, 2014.

Knowles, George. "S. L. MacGregor Mathers (1854–1918)." Controverscial. Accessed May 23, 2022. https://www.controverscial.com /Samuel%20Liddell%20Macgregor%20Mathers.htm.

Kynes, Sandra. *Llewellyn's Complete Book of Correspondences: A Comprehensive & Cross-Referenced Resource for Pagans & Wiccans.* Woodbury, MN: Llewellyn Publications, 2013.

LeFae, Phoenix. *Hoodoo Shrines and Altars: Sacred Spaces in Conjure and Rootwork.* Forestville, CA: Missionary Independent Spiritual Church, 2015.

———. *What Is Remembered Lives: Developing Relationship with Deities, Ancestors & the Fae.* Woodbury, MN: Llewellyn Publications, 2019.

———. *Witches, Heretics & Warrior Women: Ignite Your Rebel Spirit through Magick & Ritual.* Woodbury, MN: Llewellyn Publications, 2022.

LeFae, Phoenix, and Gwion Raven. *Life Ritualized: A Witch's Guide to Honoring Life's Important Moments.* Woodbury, MN: Llewellyn Publications, 2021.

Lipp, Deborah. *The Elements of Ritual: Air, Fire, Water & Earth in the Wiccan Circle.* Woodbury, MN: Llewellyn Publications, 2003.

Mankey, Jason. "All About Cakes and Ale (or Cakes and Wine)." Pathos. *Raise the Horns* (blog). November 12, 2019. https://www.patheos.com /blogs/panmankey/2019/11/cakes-ale/.

———. *The Witch's Athame: The Craft, Lore & Magick of Ritual Blades.* Woodbury, MN: Llewellyn Publications, 2016.

———. *The Witch's Book of Shadows: The Craft, Lore & Magick of the Witch's Grimoire.* Woodbury, MN: Llewellyn Publications, 2017.

———. *Witch's Wheel of the Year: Rituals for Circles, Solitaries & Covens.* Woodbury, MN: Llewellyn Publications, 2019.

Mankey, Jason, and Laura Tempest Zakroff. *The Witch's Altar: The Craft, Lore & Magick of Sacred Space.* Woodbury, MN: Llewellyn Publications, 2018.

McColman, Carl. *Before You Cast a Spell: Understanding the Power of Magic.* Franklin Lakes, NJ: New Page Books, 2004.

McCoy, Edain. *Sabbats: A Witch's Approach to Living the Old Ways.* St. Paul, MN: Llewellyn Publications, 1994.

McMahon, Mary. "What Are the Greek Classical Elements?" Cultural World. Updated July 3, 2022. https://www.wise-geek.com/what-are -the-greek-classical-elements.htm.

Melissa. "Invoking and Banishing Pentagrams." *Three Hundred and Sixty-Six* (blog), January 8, 2013. https://threehundredandsixtysix.word press.com/2013/01/08/invoking-and-banishing-pentagrams/.

Mickaharic, Draja. *Spiritual Cleansing: A Handbook of Psychic Protection.* San Francisco: Red Wheel/Weiser, 2012.

Miller, Jason. *The Elements of Spellcrafting: 21 Keys to Successful Sorcery.* Newburyport, MA: Red Wheel/Weiser, 2017.

Moura, Ann. *Grimoire for the Green Witch: A Complete Book of Shadows.* St. Paul, MN: Llewellyn Publications, 2003.

Mueller, Mickie. *The Witch's Mirror: The Craft, Lore & Magick of the Looking Glass.* Woodbury, MN: Llewellyn Publications, 2020.

Nicholas, Chani. *You Were Born for This: Astrology for Radical Self-Acceptance.* New York: HarperOne, 2020.

O'Connor, J. J., and E. F. Robertson. "Pythagoras of Samos." Mac Tutor. Accessed May 23, 2022. https://mathshistory.st-andrews.ac.uk /Biographies/Pythagoras/.

Orapello, Christopher, and Tara-Love Maguire. *Besom, Stang & Sword: A Guide to Traditional Witchcraft, the Six-Fold Path & the Hidden Landscape.* Newburyport, MA: Red Wheel/Weiser, 2018.

Regardie, Israel. *The Golden Dawn: The Original Account of the Teachings, Rites, and Ceremonies of the Hermetic Order.* Edited by John Michael Greer. Woodbury, MN: Llewellyn Publications, 2015.

"Spirit of the Sauna." Finland Philosophy. Accessed May 23, 2023. https://www.finlandphilosophy.com/en-ww/spirit-of-the-sauna.aspx.

Starhawk. *The Empowerment Manual: A Guide for Collaborative Groups.* British Columbia, Canada: New Society Publishers, 2011.

Thwaite, Annie. "A History of Amulets in Ten Objects." *Science Museum Group Journal*, no. 11 (Spring 2019). http://journal.sciencemuseum.ac.uk/browse/issue-11/a-history-of-amulets-in-ten-objects/.

Webster, Richard. *Rituals for Beginners: Simple Ways to Connect to Your Spiritual Side*. Woodbury, MN: Llewellyn Publications, 2016.

Zakroff, Laura Tempest. *Anatomy of a Witch: A Map to the Magical Body*. Woodbury, MN: Llewellyn Publications, 2021.

———. *The Witch's Cauldron: The Craft, Lore & Magick of Ritual Vessels*. Woodbury, MN: Llewellyn Publications, 2017.

Index

C

H

herbs, 16, 20, 66, 71, 81, 82, 94, 98, 99

Hermetic Order of the Golden Dawn, 6, 16, 63, 64, 75, 76, 112, 115, 116

holy water, 101, 102

horn, 2, 74

horseshoe, 90

Hoyt's Cologne, 103

I

Imbolc, 50, 187, 209, 231

incense, 1, 32, 39, 61, 62, 68, 70-72, 77, 79, 81, 92, 94, 95, 98, 99, 116, 152, 198, 208, 211-214

initiation, 4, 6-8, 57, 66, 70, 128, 170, 231

intentions, 2, 9, 13, 15, 34-36, 38, 45, 68, 94, 106, 108-110, 118, 125, 127, 132, 139, 142, 143, 171, 173, 184, 187, 196, 198, 199, 201, 205, 208-210, 216

invoke, 79, 80, 110, 113-115, 118, 123, 124, 146, 148, 150, 213, 214, 231

J

journaling, 23, 29, 32, 65, 67, 188, 191, 194, 209-211

journey, 131

Jupiter, 42, 46, 49, 53, 55, 83-86, 88, 89

K

Kelley, Edward, 112

knots, 70, 91, 92

know thyself, 21, 23, 25, 160, 192

L

labyrinth, 128

Lammas, 188, 191, 231

lavender, 85, 99

Law of Attraction, 26, 27

Leland, Charles, 6

Leo, 46-48, 53-55, 58, 83-86, 88, 89, 117, 178, 184, 185

Libra, 47, 49, 53-55, 58, 83-86, 88, 89, 179, 184, 185

lighting, 38, 141, 143, 144

T

U

To Write to the Author

If you wish to contact the author or would like more information about this book, please write to the author in care of Llewellyn Worldwide Ltd. and we will forward your request. Both the author and publisher appreciate hearing from you and learning of your enjoyment of this book and how it has helped you. Llewellyn Worldwide Ltd. cannot guarantee that every letter written to the author can be answered, but all will be forwarded. Please write to:

Phoenix LeFae
℅ Llewellyn Worldwide
2143 Wooddale Drive
Woodbury, MN 55125-2989

Please enclose a self-addressed stamped envelope for reply,
or $1.00 to cover costs. If outside the U.S.A., enclose
an international postal reply coupon.

Many of Llewellyn's authors have websites with additional
information and resources. For more information,
please visit our website at http://www.llewellyn.com.